LETTER
by
Letter

LETTER

by

Letter

AN ALPHABETICAL MISCELLANY

Laurent Pflughaupt

Princeton Architectural Press, New York

Published by
Princeton Architectural Press
37 East Seventh Street
New York, New York 10003

For a free catalog of books, call 1.800.722.6657.
Visit our web site at www.papress.com.

First published in France under the title *Lettres Latines* by Les Éditions Alternatives.
Copyright © 2003 Laurent Pflughaupt. English edition published by arrangement with
Les Éditions Alternatives, represented by Sea of Stories, www.seaofstories.com. This
edition has been adapted from the French original.

Translation: Gregory Bruhn
Editor, English edition: Nicola Bednarek
Designer, original edition: Pascal Sauvestre
Designer, English edition: Jan Haux

Special thanks to: Nettie Aljian, Sara Bader, Dorothy Ball, Janet Behning, Kristin
Carlson, Becca Casbon, Penny (Yuen Pik) Chu, Russell Fernandez, Pete Fitzpatrick,
Wendy Fuller, Clare Jacobson, Aileen Kwun, Nancy Eklund Later, Linda Lee, Aaron Lim,
Laurie Manfra, Katharine Myers, Lauren Nelson Packard, Jennifer Thompson, Arnoud
Verhaeghe, Paul Wagner, Joseph Weston, and Deb Wood of Princeton Architectural Press
—Kevin C. Lippert, publisher

Library of Congress Cataloging-in-Publication Data
Pflughaupt, Laurent, 1964–
[Lettres latines. English]
Letter by letter : an alphabetical miscellany / Laurent
Pflughaupt.
   p.   cm.
Includes bibliographical references and index.
ISBN 978-1-56898-737-8 (alk. paper)
1. Writing—History. 2. Alphabet—History. 3. Paleography, Latin.
4. Latin language—Alphabet. I. Title.
P211.P5513 2008
411—dc22
                                                                    2007037015

TABLE OF CONTENTS

For my parents.
For Sandrine & Garance.

INTRODUCTION

Dictionaries have always fascinated me. My enjoyment stems from the paths to knowledge they open before me. Dictionaries document not only the meaning of words and their evolution over the centuries, but also encapsulate within a few definitions the new realms of knowledge and techniques that emerge along the course of their publication. My personal preference has always been for illustrated works. Reading as well as looking. Drawings, paintings, photographs, and graphics this visual pleasure fuels a desire to understand, innocently inscribing an image into your memory, always leaving a trace. The letters themselves become images. Through their antiquated shapes, elegant initials, and their illuminated, rounded, or angled capitals, they create a rhythm of alternating tensions. Among the works that I have on hand, only the oldest linger over the multiple meanings and shapes that each of our letters has known over the ages. Today's dictionaries no longer do this, undoubtedly under pressure to delve directly into the heart of the matter. How then can we learn about the origin of these characters, their appearance in the ninth century, or their function as abbreviating items? As a calligrapher who is passionate for signs and respectful of letters, I wanted to bridge this gap; as a non-historian, I was unaware of how difficult that mission would prove.

So many previously unimagined directions opened up before me. The information that I was researching could not be found in any one book but in numerous works that ranged in topic from paleography, history, phonetics, and graphic arts to esotericism and philosophy. Readers should therefore not be surprised to find themselves following each of these seemingly distant paths, which in fact lead toward the same goal: inciting further research by consulting other texts, such as those listed in the bibliography.

Let us begin by analyzing two French terms, *main* (hand) and *écrire* (to write), that are particularly important in the world of signs and that we still recognize in English words such as *manual, manuscript, script,* and *scribe.* Their etymologies alone are quite significant to the spirit with which I initiated this book.

The French word *main*, which forms the second syllable of the word *humain* (human) is derived from the Latin *manus*, which is itself constructed from the Indo-European root *m-n*. This same root plays into the formation of the Latin term *mens* (intelligence or mind) and the English word *man*. Beyond what it represents—the hand—therefore, it seems that the word *main* recalls in its very essence the fundamental interactions that exist between mind and body. This fact was underscored in the fifth century BCE by the Greek philosopher Anaxagoras, who claimed: "Man is intelligent because he has hands." In fact, for thousands of years, man's attention was focused on his hands, patiently educating them in order to refine their movement. Thanks to this effort, humans eventually succeeded in fashioning the objects that would be indispensable for survival and for mastering fire. About 30,000 years before the Common Era, they started affixing signs and images to certain cave walls. This allowed for the communication of values they wished to transmit over time and space. By accomplishing this gesture, mankind took its first step toward writing.

Aside from their meaning, which escapes us to this day, wall paintings such as those found at Lascaux in France or Altamira in Spain prove that our distant ancestors had succeeded in establishing subtle links between the brain, eyes, and hands, in other words, between the three organs implicated in the act of writing. Certain rock paintings represent hands "in negative," their outlines produced by crushing color around a hand placed against the wall. Of the majority of those analyzed at Pech Merle (Lot) and Gargas (Hautes-Pyrénées) in France or at El Castillo in Spain, a few seem incomplete, with certain fingers missing.

To explain these representational differences, two hypotheses have been advanced. The first maintains that the non-represented fingers were amputated; the other proposes that it was more a question of purposefully bending certain fingers to reproduce the silent communication of hunters. The gestural and therefore fleeting transmission of information found itself fixed in representation. Charged in this way with meaning, the hand became a means of communication, lending its form to humanity's first signatures.

The word *écrire* comes from the Latin *scribere*, itself derived from the Indo-European root *ker* or *sker*, which is tied to the notion of cutting or incision. Writing would therefore suggest the fixing of any concept by means of engraved signs and not merely, as most dictionaries would have us believe, "representing a word or thought through prescribed graphic signs."

Etymologically, the term *écriture* (script) therefore lends its signification to any form of intentional representation using images or signs,
not just writing. It is applied, for example, to notation in music and
choreography.

Letters, on the other hand, have phonetic values that make them indissociable from speech and its graphic representations. Together, they
form words and phrases. Tracing back through the history of these abstract signs, which we manipulate and decipher unconsciously on a daily
basis, is often like discovering their hidden or forgotten meanings. We
find that today we still use capital letters whose structures are identical
to the engraved capitals that date from the beginning of this era. We also
discover that the design of our printed letters is based on Carolingian
lowercase letters, which were rehabilitated and perfected seven centuries
later by Florentine humanists.

Today, we know that the arrival of photography in the world of images
did not put an end to the flourishing of painting, as was once assumed. In
fact, photography favored an evolution toward new modes of expression.
While the development of printing—a veritable cultural revolution—did
not change man's relation to the act of writing, the same cannot be said
of the computer revolution. The rapid extension of networks—enhanced
with sound, image, and movement—is being carried out to the detri-
ment of writing, both in its orthographic and gestural values. In order to
rediscover its authenticity and the values that form its power, writing must
have its turn at exploring new directions.

Revealing the fundamental characteristics of writing (rhythm, relation to the body, readability, meaning), the study and practice of calligraphy constitutes an essential basis for this new direction since it encourages
the integration of skills and gestures that are indispensable to all future
forms of creativity. Far from limiting itself to the simple act of copying,
the art of beautiful writing is slowly wresting itself from the shackles of
the past. Thus, this discipline, which today integrates the techniques and
tendencies of modern graphic creation, is considered among the most
promising paths.

Indeed, the rebirth of writing has already begun in full force. In the
workaday world (and that of leisure) word-processing software offers its
users numerous typographical choices. Courses in calligraphy (Latin, Arabic, Tibetan, Chinese, etc.) are becoming increasingly common, and on
our city walls, graffiti tags bear witness to a new life for letters and symbols.

We have not reached the end of writing. In the filigree of the manuscript letter, we find our conscience inscribed. Our impulses and moods are the trace of its outline. As long as letters carry forward a part of human essence, we must continue to interrogate their mystery and beauty.

This book is conceived in homage to letters.

ORGANIZATION

The main part of this book—chapter III—is arranged in alphabetical order, letter by letter, allowing for focused consultation. Each letter is discussed through three types of analysis: The first consists in describing the different stages that punctuate its history; the second in interpreting the letter's various forms based on symbolism and graphic arts (shape analysis, color). Here, in order to best perceive each letter's design, it is useful to place as much importance on the black outline that structures it as on the counterforms (the white spaces) that help define its expression. In the third stage the various abbreviations and expressions connected with each letter are discussed, revealing a part of the letter's hidden meanings to us.

The first two chapters focus on the history and forms of the signs of the alphabet. A glossary at the end of the book offers a definition for most of the terms used, and timelines and marginal images allow us to visualize the letters during the various eras, so that we may appreciate their successive metamorphoses.

The study of the Latin alphabet developed in this book is based on correspondences, on symbolic play, and on elements borrowed from different fields of study. The originality of this approach, in which the letter itself, through its history, shape, and sound, binds together the various approaches, allows the reader to rediscover the meaning of words, not in a new light, but in a light that has been long forgotten.

NOTE

In this book, most of the letters are presented in the purified forms that they have acquired in certain typefaces. You should keep in mind that each representation is merely an "intermediary state" within a broader evolution. As a result, we are interested in those letters that fix space for a moment before then rejoining a constant recreation of form, resting on the invention of new tools, the use of new materials, the tastes of a given era, and the inspiration of typographers.

1 HISTORY

ΓΡΑΜΜΑΤΕΥΣΠΟΥ

The word *scribe* in cuneiform.

[I] The UGARITIC ALPHABET, etched on a small terracotta tablet, fourteenth century BCE.

Hieroglyph representing a scribe's tools. From left to right: a case for storing quills, a sack containing pigments, and two small pots, one for red ink, the other for black.

CUNEIFORM

Derived from the Latin *cuneus* (corner, wedge, or ankle), the term *cuneiform* refers to ancient Sumerian writing characterized by "nail-shaped" or "wedge-shaped" signs. These were imprints made in wet clay with a pointed instrument made from reeds. Once marked, the tablets, which were the primary medium for writing at that time, were dried in the sun and sometimes baked to ensure the long life of certain texts.

Appearing at the end of the fourth millennium BCE, cuneiform writing, originally transcribing Sumerian, was also used to write down other languages, such as Akkadian (2330 BCE) and Babylonian (1760 BCE). On average, it required the use of 600 signs (660 by 2300 BCE) for its ideographic and syllabic forms. One of the most famous texts written in this way is the *Epic of Gilgamesh* (around 1700 BCE), which already evokes the Great Flood.

Three centuries later, along the Syrian coast, in Ugarit (currently Ras Shamra), a city located not far from Byblos, an alphabet was born. It was composed of thirty letters (plus a separator for vertical words). The signs of the Ugaritic alphabet,[I] still in cuneiform, acquired a strictly phonetic and abstract value.

HIEROGLYPHS

The first traces of hieroglyphic script (small inscriptions on stones and pottery) date from the end of the fourth millennium BCE, at the start of the Dynastic Period. Longer texts, needed to expose the structure of Egyptian writing, did not appear, however, until the beginning of the Ancient Empire, around 2650 BCE. Hieroglyphs (from the Greek *hieros*, "sacred," and *glyphein*, "to carve") fall into three groups: logograms (representing a word), phonograms (marking a sound), and determinatives (showing the domain of application for the accompanying word). Phonograms, in turn, incorporate three types of signs: uniliteral, biliteral, and triliteral, meaning that they represent one, two, and three letters, respectively. The uniliteral signs, about thirty characters each representing a single consonant, are considered the letters of the hieroglyphic alphabet.

Thoth, the god with the head of an ibis, guardian of knowledge and writing.

The Rosetta Stone (dated March 27, 196 BCE), bearing the name of the city where it was discovered, along the west branch of the Nile. This stone made it possible for Jean-François Champollion to untangle the mystery of hieroglyphics in 1822.

A form of cursive script called *demotic* (from the Greek term *demos*, "people"), was developed early in the eighth century BCE. The text of one of Ptolemy V's decrees is engraved in demotic script at the center of the Rosetta Stone. Above and below it, the same text is transcribed into hieroglyphic and Greek scripts.

THE PROTO-SINAITIC ALPHABET

The name of this alphabet is derived from the geographical region where it was discovered, among the turquoise mines of the Sinai Peninsula (Serabit el-Khadim, see map). Even though the first Proto-Sinaitic inscriptions still pose a problem, we can reasonably situate their emergence around 1700 BCE. This alphabet would have had between twenty-three and twenty-seven signs, some of them very similar to Egyptian hieroglyphs. They most likely served as the basis for the Phoenician alphabet system.

THE PHOENICIAN ALPHABET

The first traces of this alphabet were discovered south of Ugarit, more precisely at Byblos (north of Beirut). Its appearance dates between 1100 and 1050 BCE. The oldest inscription found to date decorates the sarcophagus of Ahiram,[2] one of the kings of Byblos. That epitaph, dating from the year 1000 BCE, consists of perfectly arranged and mastered signs, and we can therefore assume that the development of this system of writing dates from a much earlier period. Writing was composed from right to left.

The sequence LAMEDH, BETH, AYIN, LAMEDH, TETH: "for the goddess Baalat."

Detail from an inscription on the sarcophagus of King Eshmunazar (fifth century BCE). Below, an inscription from King Ahiram's tomb.

2

The linear Phoenician alphabet consists of twenty-two letters, all of which are consonants and follow an order similar to the Ugaritic alphabet mentioned above. The Phoenician alphabet is particularly important because it served as the basis for the subsequent development of numerous other alphabets. In the East, it was a model for the Aramaic alphabet (and therefore the Hebraic alphabet) as well as for Arabic and Indian writing. In the West, it gave rise to the Greek alphabet, from which not only Etruscan and Latin derive, but also Cyrillic. According to the Greeks, who call their set of letters the *Kadmeia grammata* or *Phoinikea grammata* (Cadmean or Phoenician letters), the invention of the alphabet stems from the Phoenicians.

THE GREEK ALPHABET

The Greeks adopted the Phoenician alphabet toward the middle of the eighth century BCE. According to Herodotus, Cadmus (in Greek mythology the son of the Phoenician king of Tyre) brought the Phoenician alphabet, which, like other Semitic systems, was based on consonants, to the Greeks after searching for his sister, Europa, who had been abducted by Zeus. In order to adapt this system of writing to their language, the Greeks needed to create letters representing vowels. This was done by giving a vocal quality to those Phoenician consonants that were not needed to transcribe the Greek language. More precisely, the Greek alphabet was based on the Canaanite model of the Phoenician alphabet, which had twenty-two letters, from ALEPH to TAW. Three—DIGAMMA [w], SAN [s], and QOPPA [q]—were subsequently dropped, while five new signs were added after TAU: UPSILON (Y), PHI (Φ), CHI (X), PSI (Ψ), and OMEGA (Ω), which marked a long O. Thus in 403 BCE, when it was officially adopted by the city of Athens, the eastern alphabet (called *Ionian*) included twenty-four letters.

Inscriptions prior to the sixth century BCE could be written from right to left, left to right, or boustrophedon (alternating direction by line). Starting from the year 500 BCE, writing was systematically composed from left to right.

The Gezer Calendar: Written in Phoenician script, this is the oldest known Hebraic inscription, dating from 950 BCE.

Greek coin with the profile of the philosopher Democritus.

The Phoenician consonants ALEPH, HE, HETH, YODH, AYIN, and WAW became the Greek vowels: ALPHA [a], EPSILON [short e], ETA [open e], IOTA [i], OMICRON [o], and UPSILON [y, ü].

The Greek letter XI (derived from the Phoenician SAMEKH) was originally written:

It was not until the third century BCE that it appeared in the form Ξ.

ΓΡΑΜΜΑΤΕΥΣΠΟΥ
ϹΥΝΖΗΤΗΤΗϹΤΟΥ
ΑΙϢΝΟϹΤΟΥΤΟΥ
ΟΥΧΙΕΜϢΡΑΝΕΝ
ΟΘϹΤΗΝϹΟΦΙΑΝ
ΤΟΥΚΟϹΜΟΥΤΟΥΤΟΥ·
ΕΠΙΔΗΓΑΡΕΝΤΗϹΟ
ΦΙΑΤΟΥΘΥΟΥΚΕΓΝ·
ὁΚΟϹΜΟϹΔΙΑΤΗ·
ϹΟΦΙΑϹΤΟΝΘΝΕΙ
ΔΟΚΗϹΕΝΟΘϹΔΙ
ΑΤΗϹΜϢΡΙΑϹΤΟΥ

Extract from the *Codex Sinaiticus*.

B G D O

The letters B, G, D, and O were
not used in Etruscan texts.

DIGAMMA represented the [f]
sound. Its shape may result from
a graphical contraction of the
letters ꜰ and ʙ.

An ivory tablet recovered
in Marsiliana d'Albegna; it
is located at the Florence
archeological museum.

Among the subsequent forms of Greek script, we should
lend particular attention to one that appeared during the
third century CE, known as BIBLICAL MAJUSCULE. The *Codex
Sinaiticus*, a Bible produced at the Saint Catherine Monastery (located on Mount Sinai) around the middle of the
fourth century, is a perfect example of that script, which is
also called BIBLICAL UNCIAL. The letters were almost as wide
as they were tall and showed a strong contrast between the
thick stems and finer bars. This indicates that the calamus tip
was not angled to the horizontal line.

THE ETRUSCAN ALPHABET

The Etruscans settled in Tuscany beginning in the eighth century BCE. Even though many of their documents have sur-
vived, we are still unable to fully decipher their language. We
do know, however, thanks to the alphabets and texts decorat-
ing a large number of Etruscan objects (mirrors, cups, vases,
jugs, flasks, etc.) that they held their writing in high esteem.
Beyond its decorative function, it must have had importance
for them as a sign of power, education, magic, etc. The discov-
ery of writing tools (tablets, styli) in various funerary chambers
supports that theory. Based on the archaic Western-style Greek
alphabet, Etruscan script was most often read from right to left,
more rarely boustrophedon. Surprisingly, four letters of their
alphabet—B, G, D, and O—were never used in their texts.

A complete alphabet, engraved from right to left, is found
on a pendentive recovered at Marsiliana d'Albegna. This small
ivory tablet dates back to 650 BCE; its empty rectangular space

would have been covered in wax that could be engraved with the help of a stylus. The twenty-six letters along the top border served as a writing model.

Here are five signs that were used for numbers:

The number 63 (reading from right to left).

In the seventh century BCE, the Romans took inspiration from Etruscan writing in order to form their own alphabet.

THE LATIN ALPHABET

The Latin alphabet developed from the western Greek and Etruscan alphabets. A black stone found in the Roman Forum (known as the Lapis Niger) is among the oldest known Latin inscriptions, dating to the middle of the sixth century BCE. Initially composed of twenty-one letters, later twenty-four, the Latin alphabet today includes twenty-six letters, divided into twenty consonants and six vowels.

The Lapis Niger from the Roman Forum.

Archaic Latin writings were read either boustrophedon or from right to left. It was only at the beginning of the fourth century BCE that the inverse became the norm. Engraved capitals were formed in strokes of uniform thickness and did not yet have serifs. The latter, meant to reinforce the base of each

An inscription on Trajan's Column, erected in the year 113 CE.

Folium

Above, the word *folium* (leaf) in RUSTICA CAPITAL (first century). Below, fifth-century RUSTICA. The quill tip was held at a 70-degree angle, which resulted in fine stems and thick bars.

The words *laetitia* (lightness, joy) and *bonus* (good) in ROMAN CURSIVE, third century.

3 Pompeian graffiti, first century.

An example of third-century EPITOME.

sign and to improve their visual alignment, first appeared in the second century BCE. These are what characterize ROMAN MAJUSCULE, also known as "classic."

The diversification of writing tools and writing media led to a modification of letter shapes, even though scribes continued to imitate the style of engraved capitals on parchment and papyrus. These changes are notable in RUSTICA and QUADRATA, which in turn lent their graphic particularities to letters engraved in stone. Cursive writing does not appear in the Roman world until the beginning of the first century CE. At first composed solely of capital letters, little by little lowercase letters were integrated, fully supplanting the original uppercase letters in the fourth century. Cursive, which appears on media as varied as papyrus, wax tablets, and walls, was written quickly and, as a result, less carefully than the types of writing mentioned above.3

Two other scripts have been of particular interest to paleographers. The first, DE BELLIS, appears on a parchment fragment known as *De bellis macedonicis*, which dates from the first century (see P). The second is called EPITOME after a document by the same name written on papyrus (third century). Here, the distinction between thick and fine lines indicates that the quill tip was held more horizontally than for DE BELLIS. These two types of writing include letters whose forms demonstrate a subtle change between uppercase

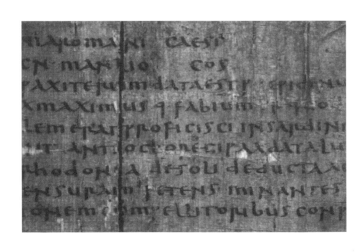

and lowercase letters. They are grouped under the denomination *mixed scripts*.

QUADRATA

This style of writing developed toward the end of the fourth century. Its design, similar to that of RUSTICA, is difficult to execute, requiring numerous manipulations of the quill. With the tip held horizontally, fine lines and thick stems were created, except in the letter R (characteristic of this writing style), which has a fine and slightly slanted stem.

Among the rare codices written in QUADRATA is the codex known as Vaticanus 3256, preserved in the Vatican library.

Fragment of *De bellis macedonicis* on parchment, first century.

LABOR

The word *labor* (work), from a text by Virgil; *Codex Vaticanus 3256*.

The letter G in QUADRATA.

QUADRATA shares two points in common with RUSTICA: the A lacks a crossbar, and there is no separation between words (*scriptio continua*).

SEMI-UNCIAL, which appears at the beginning of the sixth century, is derived from the EPITOME style and similarly includes both uppercase and lowercase letters. The significant thickening of the upper part of the stem is due to a double quill stroke, the first one rising and the second descending. Unlike what we find with RUSTICA, the stems are wide and the bars narrow, which indicates a change in how the writing tool's tip was slanted. For SEMI-UNCIAL, it forms a 15-degree angle with the horizontal.

locoadnomanorpe
ttuppano percat
bonummihioperat
mortem congutr
oriburubidattredp
noncognouiniriper

SEMI-UNCIAL.

THE UNCIALS (*littera uncialis*)

The Latin word *uncialis* means "the twelfth" and represented an ounce or an inch, depending on whether it was used to denote weight or length. An *uncialis* measured either one twelfth of the Roman pound (between 380 and 550 grams depending on the region), or of the foot. It could therefore refer here to the particularly large size of the letters (an

QVODETERNA

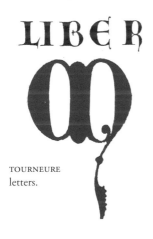

OMNESDESEDI
LJASUASURÇAN
OBHONOREM
ETREUERENTJ
AMSCÆTRINJ
TATIS·CODICES
AUTEMLECAN
TURINUIÇILAS
TAMUETERJS
TESTAMENTJ
QUAMONOUJOJ
UJNAEAUCTORJ
TATIS·SEDETEX
POSITJONESEA

With the quill angled between 0 and 20 degrees, the body of the letter is three to five times the width of the quill.

LIBER

TOURNEURE letters.

uncialis corresponds to 1.06 inches) or to the amount of gold needed for their outline.

UNCIAL script, made up of wide, rounded uppercase letters, was used mainly from the fourth to eleventh centuries for transcribing deluxe editions.

Here are some examples of these rather unique letters:

And specific ligature types:

The term includes three distinct families of letters: ROMAN UNCIALS, CLASSIC UNCIALS (sixth and seventh centuries), and ARTIFICIAL UNCIALS, also known as LATE UNCIALS (from the seventh to ninth centuries). Unlike the previous two, this last type includes pronounced serifs and initial strokes (*apices*) that required complex quill strokes.

During the Carolingian period, the UNCIALS were used as capital letters for chapter headers. (The term *capital* comes from the Latin word *caput*, "head.") Later, they lent their structure and forms to the TOURNEURE letters (ornamental capital letters) that decorate Gothic manuscripts.

CAROLINGIAN MINUSCULE
Edited between 772 and 780, the Bible known as the Abbot Maurdramne Bible—after the head of the Corbie Abbey in northern France—is the oldest known document written in CAROLINGIAN MINUSCULE, also called CAROLINE MINUSCULE. Its letter design is related to the SEMI-UNCIAL, but the letters are smaller in size, the strokes more supple, and the ligatures more frequent.

Aware of the determinative and unifying role that writing can play, Charlemagne (*Carlos Magnus*) decreed the official use of this lowercase, which bears his name, in 789.

inaegyptoerat

In aegypto erat, "It was in Egypt." The quill angle here is 35 to 40 degrees. The lowercase height is three-and-a-half times the width of the quill.

From 796 to 806, the Anglo-Saxon abbot Alcuin, head of the Saint-Martin-de-Tours Monastery, had a remarkable number of works re-transcribed into CAROLINGIAN MINUSCULE. His successor, Abbot Frédégise, continued to refine this script, and CAROLINE design reached perfection. Thanks to its sober forms and the care taken with the spaces between lines and words, CAROLINE MINUSCULE met with quick success, and its use extended rapidly beyond France's borders.

A few centuries later, Italian humanists, opposed to Gothic forms, were inspired by the design of this type of lowercase and used it as a model for humanistic script, also know as HUMANIST MINUSCULE or ANTIQUA.

Extract from the Grandval Bible, ninth century.

THE GOTHIC PERIOD

From 1070, the tips of quills were no longer cut perpendicularly to the quill's axis, but at an angle. This resulted in a change of letter appearance; cutting the tip at an angle brought about a significant change in the shapes of descenders. Breaks were made at the top and base of letters. Along with the growing number of abbreviations used in manuscripts, this is what characterized Gothic style. At the same time new characters emerged, such as the half-r **ꝛ**, which was originally used after the letter o. Later, it followed any letters with a right-hand bowl, such as the b or p.

PRIMITIVE GOTHIC, however, was not yet a fixed script. It has several points in common with CAROLINGIAN MINUSCULE, from which it derived, and the two are sometimes confused. It only became fully distinguishable from its ancestor between the thirteenth and sixteenth centuries, when it gave birth to TEXTURA, ROTUNDA, BATARDE, CURSIVE, and FRAKTUR, which are all grouped under the term *Gothic*. The angle of the quill tip to the horizontal is

Above, TEXTUS PRESCISUS VEL SINE PEDIBUS, a TEXTURA "without feet." Below, TEXTUS QUADRATUS.

Juan de Yciar's ROTUNDA.

Above, GOTHIC CURSIVE. Right, BATARDE, sixteenth century.

Above, GOTHIC FRAKTUR. Right, an extract from the 42-Line Bible.

more pronounced than the angle used to write CAROLINGIAN MINUSCULE. In Gothic scripts, it is most often at 45 degrees, creating horizontal and vertical lines of equal thickness.

Between 1452 and 1456, Johannes Gutenberg printed a Bible called "the 42-Line Bible." The font he used completely imitates the manuscript writing of that period: GOTHIC TEXTURA, more precisely known as TEXTUS QUADRATUS.

HUMANISTIC ROUND (*littera antiqua*)

The first humanist who voiced his opposition to Gothic forms was Petrarch (1304–1374). In a 1366 text addressed to his friend, the writer Giovanni Boccaccio, Petrarch denounces the weakness of Gothic script in the following terms: "this inconsistent and exuberant writing that is the privilege of scribes or, better, of painters of our time and which harms the eyes from afar, tires them up close, as if it has been invented for different reasons than to be read." He goes on to define the nascent HUMANISTIC as "another type of writing, refined, clear, innately adapted to the eye, and in which the rules of orthography and grammar have been respected."

posse non arbitrabar: ea dicta sunt a te: nec minus pla
ne q dicuntur a græcis: uerbis aptis. Sed tempus est si
uidetur: & recta quidem ad me. Quod cum ille dixis-
set: & satis disputatum uideretur: in oppidum ad pom-
ponium perreximus omnes.
.M.T. CICERONIS DE FINIBVS BONORVM ET MALORVM
LIBER QVINTVS FELICITER EXPLICIT.
Absoluit autem scriptor postrema manu: ad.iiii.kal.iunias:
uerbi anno incarnati .m.cccc sexto.

C onditiones uero pacis
unt: Que post eius fratre
famini nepe oblitus e:

23

Above, Antonio de Mario's HUMANISTIC ROUND, 1419. Left, Poggio Bracciolini's version.

It seems that the Renaissance humanists had been searching for a form of writing that was more representative of the ideas that they were defending, one that would reconcile clarity and sobriety. Thus, early in the fifteenth century, a few Italian scribes took inspiration from the CAROLINGIAN MINUSCULE, which seemed representative of the values of Antiquity (referring to the Roman world), to craft HUMANIST script. The invention of *littera antiqua* is attributed to the Florentine Giovanni Francesco Poggio Bracciolini (1380–1459). A remarkable copyist, he maintained a close relationship with Coluccio Salutati, who, in 1402, had already transcribed a treaty, *De verecundia*, with the help of a lowercase that perfectly imitated the CAROLINGIAN style of the eleventh and twelfth centuries. Some scholars consider this the first example of HUMANISTIC ROUND. The following year, Poggio Bracciolini marvelously transcribed Cicero's *Philippicae* and *Catiline Orations* in the same script style Salutati had used. The other person who played an important role in the genesis of this style was the Florentine Niccolò Niccoli (1364–1437), who is credited with editing about a dozen prestigious manuscripts.

Sed neq; adepti sut id quod u
rut: quia ueritas idest archan
sensibus no potest comphedi:
cosilia & dispositiones illius r
na. Quod quia fieri no potuit
est passus hominem deus lume
ullo laboris effectu uagari per

The ROMAN characters used by Conrad Sweynheym and Arnold Pannartz.

The imperceptible Italianization of CAROLINGIAN MINUSCULE, which lent the characters a natural and lively appearance, was abandoned in favor of the systematic verticalization

uo ceto di uui O Nyn
to benigno & delectei
ni afflato. Io acconcia
& tranquillo timored

JENSON, 1470, based on
Sweynheym and Pannartz's
design, was copied by Francisco
Griffo at Aldus Manutius's
request in order to print
Hypnerotomachia Poliphili (The
Dream of Poliphilus) in 1499.

eloquentissimum

The Latin word *eloquentissimum*
(very elegant).

HUMANISTIC CURSIVE: Niccolò
Niccoli, 1427.

HUMANISTIC CURSIVE, Rome
1477.

of characters. Endowed with pronounced serifs, the letters
became rigorous and stable. It was at that time that the
upper part and lower loop of the g, which had generally
been open in the eighth century, became closed. The letter
V also became distinguishable from U in 1425.

In 1465, at the Subiaco Monastery, in a small town not
far from Rome, printers Conrad Sweynheym and Arnold
Pannartz took inspiration from HUMANISTIC ROUND to
create the type known as ROMAN, after its place of origin.
The uppercase of this style was based on ROMAN CAPITALS
(see page 23).

HUMANISTIC CURSIVE (*littera antiqua corsiva*)
Born from HUMANISTIC ROUND and FLORENTINE GOTHIC
CURSIVE, HUMANISTIC CURSIVE was mostly used in the fifteenth and sixteenth centuries to record diplomatic acts
and briefs issued by the Pontifical Chancellery. The first
texts in this cursive (at first upright, then leaning to the
right) were written shortly before 1420. Niccolò Niccoli
used it starting in 1423. In 1500, at the request of the great
Venetian printer Aldus Manutius (1449–1515), Francisco
Griffo engraved the first italic characters based directly on
cursive manuscripts. Baptized ALDINE, this type style, better known today as italic, was used by Manutius the following year in his edition of *Virgil*.

The sixteenth century saw the appearance of many types of italic calligraphy. Among these, two stand out, CANCELLARESCA FORMATA, which was reserved for important texts, and CANCELLARESCA CORSIVA (used by the Italian writing masters Ludovico degli Arrighi and Giambattista Palatino, among others). In the first of these two scripts, the slightly inclined letters have relatively short ascenders and descenders terminating in fine horizontal or gently angled strokes. The CORSIVA style, on the other hand, is narrower and more angular. The long letters extend more than the length of a letter above or below the writing line and terminate in curved lines. The shape of the letter g is radically different from the FORMATA version.[4]

Mastering the design of the lowercase a was important since its shape was the basis for several other letters (d, g, q), and its "inverted" form was the basis for the b and p. The dynamic and elegant look of CANCELLARESCA CORSIVA, coupled with its broad interpretability, inspired modern calligraphers who appropriated its design and altered it by enlarging the letters and accentuating its curves.

4 The letter g in FORMATA and CORSIVA.

CANCELLERESCA CORSIVA,
Ludovico degli Arrighi.
La Operina, 1522.

CONTEMPORARY CHANCELLERY,
Pascal Sauvestre.

ENGLISH STYLE

This style of writing was derived from the seventeenth-century BATARDE scripts. Its ornamental quality, its grace and finesse, contributed to its popularity throughout Europe during the following two centuries. It was called COPPERPLATE in England since it was primarily engraved on copper plates. The connected letters lean heavily to the right, forming a 54-degree angle with the horizontal. Executed with a fine quill, varying pressure was applied to change the thickness of the lines, which were heaviest in the long slant.

ENGLISH, Stirling, 1830.

abcdefoghijklmnn
opqrstuvnxyz

ROUND STYLE

Appearing in 1650, the ROUND style was long taught in schools as the model for writing. It was mostly in use during the eighteenth and nineteenth centuries.

Detail from a plate of the *Encyclopédie* (1751–66) by Denis Diderot and Jean le Rond d'Alembert.

NEW DIRECTIONS

Contrary to what was suggested at the time, the development of photographic techniques did not have any negative consequences on painting. Freed from its figurative functions, painting was instead considerably enriched in its search for new forms of expression. Similarly, the spread of the printing press never extinguished the desire to write by hand and to shape letters. Today, in fact, apart from standard writing and contemporary calligraphy, we are seeing an emergence of new styles of handwritten expression (graffiti, tagging, etc.), whose forms greatly enrich our repertory of letter shapes.

Left, gestural calligraphy, David Lozach.

Calligraphers have discovered rich and promising directions by integrating manuscript forms into graphic and plastic compositions. Writing is no longer meant merely for reading but has become a veritable form of expression, loaded with new meanings and producing new values (symbols, colors, materials). "Gestural" calligraphy plays an important role in this aspect. This technique does not require any specific writing tool (you can use a brush, wood slat, drawing pen, or string) or any specific medium, and it completely embodies the notions of liveliness and rhythm. Increasing the speed of writing creates seemingly nervous letters, which are often broken up by the granular surfaces on which they are written (sidewalks, walls, watercolor paper, Ingres paper). The formal characteristics of gestural calligraphy (along with the bond it creates with the medium) lend this form a deeply modern feel.

Top, an example of "hybrid" letters. Below, a detail of contemporary calligraphy work by Laurent Pflughaupt.

TABLE OF CORRESPONDENCES

Based on a text by the English monk Bryhtferth dating from the year 1011.

Latin Alphabet	Greek Letters	Numeric Values	Semitic Letters	Latin Meanings	Possible Translations
A	Alpha	I	Aleph	*Doctevia*	The path of wisdom?
B	Bɛta	II	Bɛth	*Domus*	House, dwelling.
C	Gamma	III	Gimel	*Plenitudo*	A being's complete development.
D	Delta	IV	Delɛth	*Tabular(i)um?*	*Tabula*, board. *Tabularium* Archives.
E	Eta	V	He	*Ista*	What is yours, that one.
F	Serenon?	VI	Vav	*Et*	Coordinating conjunction, connection.
G	Zɛta	VII	Zain	*Hec*	Alteration of *hic*? Used for designating.
H	Hɛta	VIII	Eth	*Vita*	Life, existence.
	Θ thɛta	IX	Thɛth	*Bonum?*	Good.
I (J)	Iota	X	Ioth	*Principum*	Beginning, commencement, origin.
K	Kappa	XX	Caph	*Manus*	Hand.
L	λauda?	XXX	Lamech	*Disciplina*	Apprenticeship, education, science.
M	My	XL	Mem	*Ex ipsis*	From the same. Out of.
N	Ny	L	Nun	*Sempiternum*	Eternal, perpetual, endless.
	Z xi	LX	Sameth	*Adjutorium*	Aid, help, support.
O	Oa Omicron	LXX	Ain	*Fons*	Spring, fountain, origin, cause, principle.
P	Π Pi	LXXX	Phe	*Oms*	Mouth.
	M san		Sade	*Justicia*	Justice, honesty.
Q	ci.coppa	XC	Coph	*Vocatio*	Vocation (divine), invitation, calling.
R	P Ro	C	Res	*Caput*	Head.
S	Css ma	CC	Sin	*Dentium*	Tooth.
T	T Tau	CCC	Tau (v)	*Signa*	Signs, marks, impressions.
V (U)	Y y Upsilon	CCCC			
X	Φ ifi	D			
Y	χ chi	DC			
Z					
	Ψ Psi	DCC			
	Ω Omega	DCCC			
	ɔ Sanpi	CM			

2
FORMAL ANALYSIS

STROKES

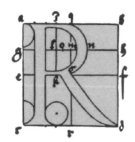

The layout for constructing a letter R, by Albrecht Dürer.

The letters' slightly concave stem creates convex spaces. On the contrary, thicker midsections create concave spaces.

[1] The horizontal line evokes rest. It is associated with the colors green and blue.

L etters, regardless of their style, are composed of a certain number of curved, straight, simple, and complex strokes, connected in specific ways. Each letter's ductus, or framework, demonstrates the order and direction of each stroke. Character strokes fall into two categories: straight lines (horizontal, vertical, and diagonal) and curved lines. The arrangement of the straight lines creates different types of angles that structure the letters. The openness of its angles gives the letter its specific characteristics. The shape and location of the empty spaces in and around a character also play a determining role in constructing this letter "identity."

STRAIGHT LINES

Symbolically, a straight line is the simplest representation of the male sex. When drawing faces and muscles, the use of straight lines tends to express the model's virility. Easy to imagine and difficult to deform (without losing its specific quality), the straight line expresses power and stability within any structured element. It may also evoke rigidity and inflexibility. That is why signs made up solely of straight lines seem mechanical and cold, poorly compatible with the human race. As a result, the noble character of straight lines only comes through when combined with curved lines. The straight line, defined as the shortest distance between two points, also evokes a sense of support and functionality.

Depending on their direction, straight lines can be classed as follows:

HORIZONTAL STROKES

These suggest no movement, except if the stroke itself reveals the direction in which it was drawn. Wassily Kandinsky, in his work entitled *Point and Line to Plane*, associated the horizontal[1] with the notion of frigid calm. Related to bodies, it represents a prone position (the position of rest); in this position, the brain no longer needs to maintain balance.

The horizontal also represents the straight line between our shoulders. In terms of writing, it is the basis for a line of text. The horizontal strokes of certain letters are called either "crossbar" (A, H) or "bar" (E, F, I, T, Z).

VERTICAL STROKES

Symbolically, vertical strokes represent the elements that link Earth and sky. They create a relationship between the forces from on high and those below, the theological *mi* and the anthropological *ma* (see M). Here, man is awake, standing, conscious. In the realm of letters, vertical strokes are called stems. This term includes downstrokes (descenders or tails), which extend below the line of writing, as well as upstrokes (ascenders), which extend above.

Kandinsky associates verticality[2] with warm calm.

THE DIRECTION OF THE STROKE

Moving from left to right, lines change in time. In the realm of writing, they move forward, drawing us along toward the rest of the text. A line drawn from right to left seems oriented toward the past, thereby evoking the idea of return. This same effect can be found in comic books, where a person looking to the right seems to be moving toward a new space, whereas looking to the left he seems to be retracing his steps.

Diagonals, since we read from left to right, seem to be either ascending or descending.

DIAGONAL STROKES

The essential characteristics of diagonal strokes stem from the fact that they imply movement. Depending on their direction, from left to right, ascending or descending, they are considered "harmonious and lyrical" (positive) or "discordant" (negative), respectively. In addition, similar to the vertical and horizontal strokes, they demonstrate "warm" or "cold" qualities, as mentioned above.

Letter strokes created on a diagonal have a different name depending on their place within the sign: arms (K and Y), upstrokes (A and V), tails (R and Q), strokes (N), and, finally, broken strokes (M). The nature of a diagonal line—its

[2] The vertical line evokes activity and alertness, even if it does not convey a notion of movement. It is associated with the colors yellow and red.

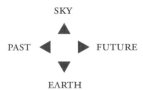

The letter loses its static quality in its italic form.

A "lyrical" diagonal line. The stroke is full of energy and implies increase.

A "discordant" diagonal line creates a feeling of diminution.

N

The stroke on the N is a "discordant" diagonal.

3 The feminine is symbolically associated with even numbers, the moon, and silver. In China, where it corresponds to *yin*, it is linked with the passive, the somber, and the internal.

TOURNEURE capital in a fourteenth-century book of hymns.

Decorative flourishes based on POETICA SUPP ORNAMENTS

shape and appearance—can finesse or even undermine its directional characteristics, in the sense that even a stroke made on a lyrical diagonal axis will seem to descend if it appears to have been drawn from bottom to top ╱ .

CURVED LINES

There is a natural correspondence between curved lines and the realm of the feminine.[3] Representing flexibility, grace, and softness, curved lines recall the maternal womb, the roundness of breasts, the silhouette of thighs, hips, and skin. They command immediate compassion since they are characteristic of the tender, playful world of children. In manuscripts, certain wavy lines recall the movement of a lock of hair or of water. Spirals and other arabesques in lighter, more elegant designs evoke images of air.

In an attempt to break from the rigor of Gothic texts, copyists used uppercase letters with particularly rounded, ample shapes, called TOURNEURES, which were meant to balance out the page with their curves.

Whereas the mental image of a straight line can be conjured immediately, it is much more difficult to imagine a curved line, since it may come in many forms. The absence of any straight, and therefore "structuring," line in a curve posed a certain number of problems for calligraphers. In the art of writing letters, curved lines are effectively more difficult to execute than straight lines. Tracing them requires a mental simplification of their design, decomposing the curve into a series of straight lines, as you would imagine a square while drawing a circle.

The ductus for a letter O[4] consists of a downward stroke, a stroke moving right (1 and 2), and then another stroke moving right followed by a downward stroke (3 and 4).

ANGLES

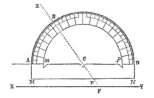

A protractor, used for measuring angles.

Angles (apart from the flat, or *null*, angle) result from the intersection of straight lines coming from different directions. They fall into three categories depending on the degree of aperture: *obtuse*, *right*, or *acute*. As mentioned above, angles are what give letters their power, structure, and specific character; the letter Z, for example, seems more aggressive than the L.

In calligraphy, the angle created by the quill's tip and the horizontal determines the layout of thicker and finer lines within each letter.

ACUTE ANGLES

More closed than a right angle, an acute angle suggests acidity (related to yellow-green), heat (yellow and red), speed, excitation, and activity. The more the angle is closed, the more aggressive it becomes. This jagged and cutting look is associated with objects that wound deeply (the blade of a knife, a shard of mirror, a needle). As their name implies, acute angles correspond to the strident (the phoneme [i]), the high, and the intense (an acute crisis). They evoke precision and finesse: a pointed analysis, a piercing eye, a heightened sense of reality. In longhand and signatures, they denote a strong will or great insistence, but may also betray a certain nervousness. This can be seen in manuscripts from the fifteenth century, written in GOTHIC BATARDE.[5] The rapidly traced letters of these texts possess a quick rhythm and impart a feeling of mastery and subtle intelligence.

THE RIGHT ANGLE

The right angle, with an opening of 90 degrees, may be considered objective and tempered. Though rarely present in nature (except in some crystalline rocks), it appears in countless human constructions (architecture, graphic arts, design). It may therefore be considered the most "human" of angles.

The triangle is associated with the color yellow and with the spiritual world.

5

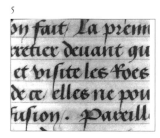

Red is associated with the square, a symbol of Earth and of matter.

The right triangle, a symbol of rectitude and construction.

The eight sides of an octagon are enough to make this polygon resemble a circle.

The right angle regulates the normative systems in which we have become used to evolving. It is practical for everything from schoolchildren's graph paper to the shapes of modern houses. The right angle's functional, structuring, and therefore economical role guarantees it a place of importance within our society.

It appears in three basic geometrical shapes: the square, the rectangle, and the right triangle and is also found in right trapezoids, which have three consecutive, perpendicular sides.

Based on their structure, there are two letters that share a close relationship with the right angle: the Greek GAMMA (Γ) and the L. The shape of the GAMMA partly explains why the letter G was an important Masonic symbol (see G). The history of the L contains the teaching and the straightness conveyed by its ancestor, the Phoenician LAMEDH, which represented a goad, or staff (see L).

The right angle instills power in letters. It is more often found in uppercase letters than in lowercase. Its perpendicular lines mirror the axes of the human body, formed between the vertebral column and the shoulders (the image of Christ on the cross).

OBTUSE ANGLES

Ranging from 90 to 180 degrees, obtuse angles seem more passive than either acute or right angles. They play a role in equilateral geometric shapes with more than four sides, such as the pentagon, the hexagon, and the decagon. The more sides a polygon has, the more it resembles the circle, thereby acquiring the circle's symbolic values: softness, femininity, colder colors (green and blue), symbols of the celestial, the spiritual, and the familial.

This type of angle emanates a feeling of fullness and calm. You can sense this, for example, in the ample design of UNCIAL letters, which are particularly open and round. The weakness of these angles is apparent from both formal and structural points of view. In fact, they prove to be relatively fragile and dull. In the field of graphic communication, they may be interpreted as a lack of assertiveness.

RECTANGLES

The perfect rectangle, or square, calls to mind notions of stability, objectivity, and rigor. Indissociable from the circle (related to the sky, the color blue, and femininity), in which it can be inscribed or which it can contain, the square is associated with the color red and with the Earth (the expression: "the four corners of the world"). In writing, it serves as the structural basis for Chinese ideograms and ROMAN MAJUSCULES.[6]

The even horizontal and vertical tension lends the square a particularly stable and reassuring posture. That quality is the reason for its frequent use in graphic arts; its structure makes logotypes and other images solid and seemingly serious. The expression "to look someone squarely in the eyes" plays on these intrinsic qualities of the square.

The nature of a rectangle is primarily determined by the relationship of its height to its width. When there is a relationship of 1.414 (or √2), a quadrilateral enters into the category known as *dynamic*, most notably represented by the golden rectangle. A relationship of √2 is used in European DIN-A paper formats (A3, A4, etc.). This formatting starts with A0 (1189 x 841 mm), which equals one square meter. This is the only measure that maintains its proportion when a sheet of paper is folded in half, which makes it particularly economical in printing. Other characteristics are dependent on its position: horizontal, vertical, or angled (see Strokes).

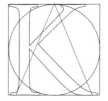

[6] The letters in the classical Roman alphabet are based on three simple geometric shapes: the circle, the triangle, and the square.

A format is called *landscape* when its width is greater than its height, and *portrait* when the reverse is true.

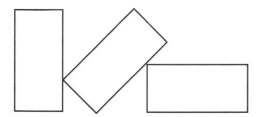

$$\Phi = \frac{1 + \sqrt{5}}{2} = 1.618$$

A growing spiral based on the golden rectangle.

A rectangle measuring
0.83 x 0.51 inches, containing
the letter L.
0.83 / 0.51 = 1.627 ≈ Φ

THE GOLDEN RECTANGLE

Among the so-called dynamic rectangles, there is one that, for centuries, has held the attention of æsthetes. It is called the golden rectangle and has a height to width ratio that perfectly matches the golden number, 1.618, represented by the Greek letter PHI (Φ), the initial of the Greek sculptor Phidias. This golden ratio is often found in nature, particularly in growing processes, such as the spiral growth patterns of pine cones or sunflowers, for example. Due to its exceptional qualities, this proportion is frequently used in the creative arts (architecture, graphic art, painting, design).

LETTER ANATOMY
STRUCTURAL ELEMENTS

T he terms *ascender* and *descender* share a common origin: the Latin word *scandere* (to climb). We use *descender* (also downstroke) for the vertical strokes that extend below the x-height of a letter and *ascender* (also upstroke) for those that extend above the x-height. *Boldness* corresponds to the thickness of a letter's strokes, *body size* corresponds to its height, and *set width* refers to the lateral dimension of a letter and its surrounding space.

The different thicknesses of BAUER BODONI. Roman, bold, and black.

CHAKRAS

I t may seem surprising to turn our attention to the notion of *chakras* in a work dedicated to Latin letters. We should keep in mind that the primary function of the letters of our alphabet is to notate the sounds inherent to our language, in other words, to represent speech. The voice requires not only breath but also movement of different parts of the body, in the form of

DIAGRAM OF VOCAL
APPARATUS

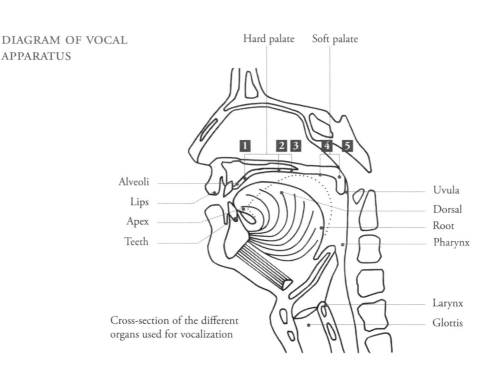

Cross-section of the different
organs used for vocalization

ORGANS	PHONEMES	ORGANS	PHONEMES
• Lips	Labials	• Uvula	Uvulars
• Teeth	Dentals	• Pharynx	Pharyngeals
• Alveoli	Alveolars	• Larynx	Epiglottals
• Hard palate (1)	Pre-palatals	• Glottis	Glottals
• Hard palate (2)	Medial palatals	• Apex	Apicolabials
• Hard palate (3)	Post-palatals	• Dorsal	Dorsals
• Soft palate (4)	Pre-velars	• Root	Radicals
• Soft palate (5)	Post-velars		

vibrations. Whereas vowels only need a free flow of breath and the vibration of the larynx, this is not the case for consonants. To form these the buccal cavity has to be opened, shortened (constrictives and fricatives), or closed (occlusives) at different points. Our phonological apparatus includes the following organs: the hard palate (and the soft palate, closer to the uvula), the uvula, the pharynx, the larynx (the primary phonic organ), the glottis, the alveoli, the teeth, the lips, and of course the tongue, which is divided into three parts: the apex (or tip), the dorsal, and the root. Consonants are categorized as dental, alveolar, dorsal, palatal, velar, pharyngeal, laryngeal, or labial depending on the organ or organs used for their pronunciation. The distinct articulation of vowels depends not only on how open the mouth is, but also where the breath comes from. With no natural obstacle along the way to exteriorization, vowels are considered particularly "pure." Therefore they garner more attention (in the realm of phonetics) than consonants, which require more "mechanistic characteristics" for pronunciation.

The English language has fifteen vowel and nineteen consonant sounds, which can be represented by numerous graphemes. For example, the [i] vowel can be expressed by such various spellings as *me, see, seat, receive, machine, people*.[6] So the twenty-six letters of the English alphabet are in fact the raw material used to create graphemes, which can consist of more than one letter.

The word *chakra* comes from Sanskrit and means "wheel." There are seven main *chakras* distributed along the spinal column and animated by a circular movement, hence their name. Conically shaped and opening outward, the *chakras* are considered energy points.[7] In India, *kundalini* is the creative force that resides in the coccyx region. It is the force known as *shakti* according to Hindu beliefs. The first *chakra* opens downward, the seventh upward, and the five others open forward.

The body is crisscrossed by a network of energy lines, called *nadis*, with the *sushumna* being the most important of them. Located within the vertebral column (spinal fluid), the *sushumna* is rooted in the coccyx, seat of the first *chakra*,

6 The two letters s and h are combined into a digraph sh to represent a single phoneme (the first sound of *shoe*, the end sound of *wash*, etc.).

7 *Shiva*: energy flowing through the body, descending from the summit along *sushumna*. *Shakti*: energy flowing from the base, ascending along the *sushumna*.

The position of the *chakras*.

TABLE
In the column "notes," the letters in parentheses correspond to the notes of the musical system of Romance countries. The last column presents the letters A to G, which were used to indicate the days of the week on older European ecclesiastical calendars and in prayer books. The A's supremacy is once again evident, since it was used as the mark of the Lord's day, Sunday.

and ends at the crown of the head, where the seventh *chakra* is located. Another important *nadis* is called *Ida*. Associated with lunar energy, it starts on the left side of the coccyx and ends at the left nostril. The *nadis* called *Pingala* starts at the right of the coccyx and ends at the right nostril. It is related to solar energy. These three *nadis* are the primary lines of this energy system.

Each *chakra* is connected to a set of organs on which it acts in a specific manner. When energy flows harmoniously between these points, this is known in India as *prana* ("absolute energy" in Sanskrit, "the vital breath") and as *chi* in China and Japan. It is a guarantee of good health. On the other hand, any dysfunction within the system (a closing or blockage) will lead to a loss of energy in the associated organs, as well as to a variety of other problems. For example, feeling your throat tighten may be the result of strong emotions and the closing off of the third *chakra*. Situated around the solar plexus, the third *chakra* is in fact connected to the diaphragm, the center of our emotions.

TABLE OF CORRESPONDENCES

7 colors (+ black and white), 7 planets, 7 metals, 7 musical notes, 7 days

COLORS	PLANETS	METALS	NOTES	DAYS	LETTERS
White	Moon	Silver	Rest	Monday	B
Violet	—	—	B (Si)	—	
Indigo	Mercury	Mercury	A (La)	Wednesday	D
Blue	Jupiter	Tin	G (Sol)	Friday	F
Green	Venus	Copper	F (Fa)	Thursday	E
Yellow	Sun	Gold	E (Mi)	Sunday	A
Orange	Sun	Gold	D (Re)	—	
Red	Mars	Iron	C (Do)	Tuesday	C
Black	Saturn	Lead	Rest	Saturday	G

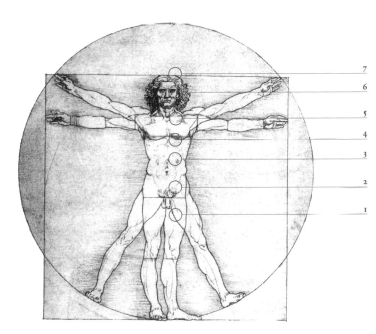

7   Crown, seventh *chakra*.

6   *Ajna*, or third eye, sixth *chakra*.

5   Throat, fifth *chakra*.

4   Heart, fourth *chakra*.

3   Solar plexus, third *chakra*.

2   *Hara* or *tan dien*, second *chakra*.

1   Perineum, first *chakra*.

LHOMME LETRE.

	NOTES	VOWELS	ELEMENTS	COLORS
seventh CHAKRA	B (Si)	M	—	Violet, white, and gold
sixth CHAKRA	A (La)	I	—	Indigo, yellow, and violet
fifth CHAKRA	G (Sol)	E	Ether	Blue
fourth CHAKRA	F (Fa)	A	Air	Green, pink, and gold
third CHAKRA	E (Mi)	O^o	Fire	Yellow, gold
second CHAKRA	D (Re)	O^c	Water	Orange
first CHAKRA	C (Do)	U	Earth	Red

In the "vowels" column, Oo stands for "open O" and Oc stands for "closed O."
M is considered a vowel here (see M). Left, the correspondences between letters
and body parts, established by Geoffroy Tory, from *Champ Fleury*.

COLORS

"Color is that part of art which is the quintessential seat of the magical gift. Whereas the subject, form, and line primarily engage thought, color is of no meaning to the intellect, but holds every power over sensitivity, it stirs up feelings."

—Eugène Delacroix

The goal here is not to develop a deep analysis of color, but simply to point out its vibrant nature, which allows us to establish a subtle correspondence between colors, various parts of the body, and the letters of the alphabet, whose pronunciation requires a series of vibrations.

Sunlight, considered white light, breaks down through a prism into seven fundamental colors located between infrared and ultraviolet: red, orange, yellow, green, blue, indigo (a dark blue gently tinged with red), and violet. Each is defined by its wavelength. The human eye is most sensitive to green, the color representing the majority of the solar rays reaching Earth. An object that appears red in fact absorbs all of the colors of the spectrum except red, which it reflects. A white piece of clothing therefore is best for dealing with heat since it reflects the whole spectrum's energy.

In this context it is interesting to note that colors only show up in the presence of light, and that the word *illumination* (miniature illustrations in illuminated manuscripts) comes from the Latin *illuminare* (to make luminous).

In his poem "Vowels," Arthur Rimbaud associates a color to each vowel, thereby emphasizing the poetic and symbolic connections that unite them.

In Paleolithic drawings, we find generally two colors: red and black. In Egypt, the ideogram representing a scribe's tools shows two pots, one for each color (see History).

The colors associated with the five Chinese elements:

Water: Black
Fire: Red
Earth: Yellow
Wood: Green
Metal: White

A noir, E blanc, I rouge, U vert, O bleu: voyelles,
Je dirai quelque jour vos naissances latentes:
A, noir corset velu des mouches éclatantes
Qui bombinent autour des puanteurs cruelles,

Golfes d'ombre; E, candeurs des vapeurs et des tentes,
Lances des glaciers fiers, rois blancs, frissons d'ombelles;
I, pourpres, sang craché, rire des lèvres belles
Dans la colère ou les ivresses pénitentes;

U, cycles, vibrements divins des mers virides,
Paix des pâtis semés d'animaux, paix des rides
Que l'alchimie imprime aux grands fronts studieux;

O, suprême Clairon plein des strideurs étranges,
Silences traversés des Mondes et des Anges;
—O l'Oméga, rayon violet de Ses Yeux!

A black, E white, I red, U green, O blue: vowels,
I will recount some day your latent births:
A, black corset furry with sparkling flies
That buzz around cruel stenches,

Gulfs of shadow; E, candor of vapors and of tents,
Proud spears of glaciers, white kings, quivering umbels;
I, purples, spit blood, laugh of beautiful lips
In rage or in repentant drunkenness;

U, cycles, divine vibrations of verdant seas,
Peace of pastures sown with livestock, peace of wrinkles
Imprinted by alchemy onto broad studied brows;

O, supreme Clarion full of foreign shrills,
Silences traversed by Worlds and by Angels:
—O the Omega, violet ray from His Eyes!

COLORS	SYMBOLIC CORRESPONDENCE	CHAKRAS	NOTES	VOWELS
VIOLET	Spirituality, religion, sadness, melancholy, triangle, darkness, dignity, affliction, softness.	Crown	Si	[m]
INDIGO	Evening, calm, serenity and rest, dreaming, softness, oval shapes.	Third eye	La	[i]
BLUE	Sky, air, sea, freshness, cold, ice, circle or sphere, horizontal, transparency.	Throat	Sol	[e]
GREEN	Sea, chlorophyll, water, respiration, relaxation, freshness, circle, nature, rebirth, femininity, humidity, calm, hope, horizontal.	Heart	Fa	[a]
YELLOW-GOLD	Sun, vitality, visibility, energy, light, radiating, divinity, triangle. YELLOW-GREEN: betrayal, jealousy, illness.	Solar plexus	Mi	[o] open
ORANGE	Dynamism, visibility, vitality (vitamin C), joy, appetite stimulation, industry.	*Hara*	Re	[o] closed
RED	Energy, dynamism, passion, love, blood, sex, fertility, heat, anger, prohibition, Earth, fire, square or cube, masculinity, solidity, power, action.	Perineum	Do	[u]

WHITE	Purity, totality, amplitude, luminosity, innocence, spirit, silence, divinity, absolute, mourning (China).	
SILVER	Moon, femininity, coldness, aquatic.	
GOLD	Sun, masculinity, heat, eternity (pure metal), divinity.	
BROWNS	Usefulness, reality, robustness, reassurance, the father, structure, construction, wood, Earth, the home, the quotidian.	
GREY	Atonal, monotony, sadness, illness, indecision, old age, neutrality.	
BLACK	Totality, nothingness, the unknown, silence, obscurity, fear, mourning, elegance, renunciation.	

CORRESPONDENCES WITH ASTROLOGICAL SIGNS:

RED: Aries
GREEN: Taurus
BROWN: Gemini
SILVER: Cancer
GOLD: Leo
MULTICOLOR: Virgo
PALE GREEN: Libra
VERMILLION: Scorpio
SKY BLUE: Sagittarius
GRAY: Aquarius
NAVY BLUE: Pisces

3

LETTER
BY LETTER

The Hebraic ALEPH

"You will be the first among letters, and I will only find unity in you; you will be the basis for every act committed in the world, and no unity will be found, except in the letter aleph." —Zohar I, 3a. The book was written in Spain in the thirteenth century but the work is ascribed to Shimon bar Yochai, a rabbi who lived during the second century.

[1] The image of a bull or ox evokes labor and domesticated force. Its name is contained in the word *boustrophedon* (from the Greek *bous*, "ox," and *strephein*, "to turn"), which refers to writing systems that alternate by line from right to left and left to right.

A

AMPLITUDE STABILITY
NOBILITY

First letter of the alphabet
& first vowel

ORIGIN & EVOLUTION

The first pictograms that evolved into the first Phoenician letter ALEPH and eventually our letter A had the form of a bull or an ox. Drawn rather realistically, the animal was represented either in its entirety or simply by the outline of its head: .[1]

In the Proto-Sinaitic alphabet, around 1700 BCE, it appeared in this form: ⟨⟩. Later simplifications present the head simply as a triangle on point, with horns protruding above. During the eleventh century BCE, the Phoenicians rotated the glyph 90 degrees, with the animal's horns now facing right.

The letter A may also be related to another animal drawn in the Egyptian hieroglyphic alphabet: the vulture. Early on, this sign transcribed the sound of the liquid consonants R and L. Its sound became increasingly shortened over time, resulting from a movement of the glottis, and today the vulture hieroglyph 𓅐 corresponds to the sound conventionally noted as: 3, ' (apostrophe), or a.

The use of the glottis, noted as ['], is the first letter of the word *aleph*, constructed on the consonant base ['lf]. Written אלף in Hebrew, this word means "cow," "bull," or "large livestock." As we can see, the Phoenician letter ALEPH is named after the word for which it is an initial and is pronounced

100		400			800	
Western Greek		De Bellis	Quadrata	Uncial		Irish Semi-uncial	Carolingian
	Roman Capital	Roman Cursive	Rustica		Artificial Uncial	Runic-style Majuscule	Tourneure

liked the first phoneme of that word. This principle of naming letters is called the *acrophonic* principle (from the Greek *akros*, "edge").

The Greeks, whose language contains more vocal variations than Semitic languages do, used the sign of the Phoenician guttural ALEPH, turned another 90 degrees, to represent a vowel in their alphabet. Passing from Phoenician into Greek, letters' names typically were only slightly altered. Thus the Semitic ALEPH became the Greek ALPHA, the basis for our word *alphabet*. The capital A in Latin alphabets is based on the shape of the Greek letter. In certain scripts, such as QUADRATA and RUSTICA, this letter was drawn without a crossbar connecting its two upstrokes, more closely resembling the Greek LAMBDA (Λ). Today, it still appears in the form of an upside-down V in certain typefaces.

The Phoenician ALEPH, from the Mesha Stele, circa 830 BCE.

The Greek letter ALPHA seems to gather force from the Earth to rise up toward the heavens. The first two shapes coexisted in the sixth century BCE. The third, with a broken crossbar, is found starting in the third century BCE.

SHAPES & INTERPRETATIONS
Through the rotation in the course of its evolution the A gained a sense of stability in its graphic interpretation. In the new configuration, the bull's horns that had once pointed to the heavens became the legs on which man stood, thereby establishing a link or a point of contact with the Earth's energies.

Left, modern interpretations. Above, UNCIAL forms.

Gothic Primitive
1200

1300	1400	1600	
Gothic Textura	Batarde	Humanistic	——— Fraktur ———
——— Rotunda ———	Gothic Cursive	Chancellery	Modern forms of various inspiration

² *Champ Fleury,
Art et science de la vraie
proportion des lettres.*

Layout of the capital based on
three simple geometric shapes:
the circle, the triangle, and
the square.

³ The four elements: air, fire,
earth, and water. The first two
are connected with masculinity,
the other two with femininity
(see V).

Two forms coexist in GOTHIC
TEXTURA.

AdAm

The name of the first man,
Adam, comes from the Hebrew
adamah, meaning "worked
earth."

Contrary to what one might think, the crossbar in the A is not located at the letter's midpoint. Its position slightly below the geometric middle reinforces the letter's strength and stability. In his work entitled *Champ Fleury,*² published in 1529, Geoffroy Tory placed the A's crossbar at the height of the genitals, a position that is near the human body's center of gravity. In ROMAN CAPITALS, the letter is shaped like a triangle pointing upward, a basic form with numerous symbolic interpretations. For the Greeks, the triangle represented balance and reason.

Today, a triangle is a symbol of spirituality. Formed by joining two points, the base represents the dichotomies of the human and earthly world; the upper part, central and solitary, implies the notion of a superior reality. It is thus not surprising to see the divine eye (or third eye) placed in the middle of such a triangle. Pointing upward, it is a symbol of the masculine, and downward, a symbol of the feminine (see V). The two forms are interlaced in the Star of David ✡, which also represents the four elements.³

In lowercase, the letter a has countless forms, which can nonetheless be grouped into two main families:
—one consists of the "closed a" sign, written **ɑ**.
—the other of the "open a" sign, written **a**.

The following forms are found in the first group:
SEMI-UNCIAL: **ɑ**, MEROVINGIAN: **ɑ**,
ANGLO-SAXON: **ɑ**, BATARDE: **a**, GOTHIC CURSIVE: **a**,
FRAKTUR: **a**, CHANCELLERY: **a**, ROUND: **a**.

And in the second:
CAROLINGIAN: **a**, TEXTURA: **a**, ROTUNDA: **a**,
HUMANISTIC: **a**.

THE LETTER'S VIBRATORY NATURE

In Hinduism and Buddhism, certain syllables and phrases are considered sacred. These are the mantras that strengthen the body's energies when vocalized. The best known syllables are *Nam-Myo-Ho-Ren-Ge-Kyo,* which mean: "Devotion to the mystic law of the lotus flower Sutra" or "Mystic order of the infinite universe."

The letter A is the basis for the mantra that encompasses the whole range of vibrations from the first *chakra* to the last: the sacred syllable *aum* (also written *om* and pronounced A-U-M), in which the [a] sound vibrates in the lower body. It contains fundamental energies that allow for the spirit to be elevated (see also U and M).

The [a] sound (pronounced as the a in *father*), when sung in the key of A, acts upon the fourth *chakra*. This is the heart *chakra*, which is associated with air and corresponds with the colors green, pink, and gold.

Pronouncing the letter A, especially when it is preceded or followed by an H, brings forth notions of amplitude and coolness as well as rapture and ecstasy. In English spelling the letter can represent various other vowel sounds as illustrated by the words *all*, *cat*, *face*, *fancy*. The [a] in *father* most closely resembles the Latin [a] sound.

The letter already had a relationship with the aquatic among the Sumerians, whose pictogram for it, ≈, represented water and was pronounced [a].

As the *Grand dictionnaire françois et latin* from 1737 states: "This vowel expresses almost the full range of our souls' movements." What is more, its simple and natural pronunciation requires no particular articulation. This is why it was baptized the "baby's vowel." The attributes given to the letter A also correspond to those associated with the color black, which Rimbaud equates with the letter.[4] Like the letter A, the color black may be qualified as noble, ample, open, perfect, grave, and stable.[5]

THE LETTER IN BRIEF, ABBREVIATIONS & MEANINGS

→ The letter's numeric value represents unity: A = 1.

→ According to the phrase recorded by the ecclesiastical historian Caesar Baronius, *possidet A numeros quingintos ordine recto,* among the Romans the value of an A shifted from 500 to 5000 when a *titulus* was placed above it: $\overline{A}$ = 5000

Expressive phrases:

AAAAH ! ha, ha ha !

4 Black absorbs every color on the luminous spectrum. Chemically, it is formed essentially from carbon, derived from animals, minerals, and vegetables. Thanks to this compound, it is highly resistant to light. Along with red, it was the earliest color used by humans.

5 See *Dictionnaire des symboles*, Éditions Bouquins.

Abbreviated *am* in the ending *tam*.

$$\alpha$$

For the Greeks, the A (or α) had a numeric value of 1.

The symbol for anarchy.

→ In Antiquity, the letter A was called the *littera salutaris*, the salutary or saving letter. During voting in tribunals, the elders placed small tablets into an urn. On each tablet was inscribed a letter, generally the first letter of a word. The letter A was an abbreviation of *absolvo* (I absolve). It indicated acquittal, grace, and pardon by the fathers. Sometimes it could also take on the meaning of *antiquo*, and therefore meant a rejection of a law. For the Greeks, on the other hand, it was the sign of a bad omen when uttered during a sacrifice.

→ The Greeks and Romans used letters to represent musical notes. A was the first note of the hyperbolic tetrachord, the lowest tone on the musical scale. During the eleventh century, when the notes were renamed UT, RE, ME, FA, SOL, LA, SI (which later became DO, RE, ME, FA, SO, LA, TI), it was noted that the A of the Ancients corresponded to the low-octave LA. As a result, the letter A became the LA tone. This notation corresponds to Anglo-Saxon and Germanic musical nomenclature (C, D, E, F, G, A, B), wherein the letter A represents the note LA.

→ In ancient treatises on chemistry, AA or AAA represents amalgam.

→ In medical ordinances, aa or ana (from the Greek *analogos*, "proportionate") means "equal parts."

→ In ancient European religious calendars, the letter A corresponds with Sunday.

→ AD is the abbreviation of *anno domini* (in the year of [our] Lord).

→ Å is the symbol for angstrom (10^{-10} meters).

→ The letter once stood for *azote,* nitrogen. This element is now represented by the letter N, from its former name *nitrum.*

→ An A in a circle is the symbol of anarchy.

→ In English, *a* is an indefinite article.

EXPRESSIONS

— From Λ to Z

— To know your ABCS

→ The letter A marks the "ace," the strongest card in the deck. A person who is regarded as the most adept in a certain field is also called an ace. The superiority of A is also evident in the academic grading scale.

→ An A-frame is a house whose shape mimics that of the letter A.

In mathematics, an upside-down A means "given any." As a universal quantifier, it means "for all."

A

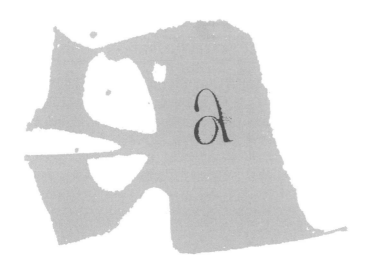

The sign is formed by contracting *a* and *ð*.

THE AT SIGN

The shape of this sign is a result of the graphic contraction of the letters a and d, forming the Latin preposition *ad*, which implies movement and direction. For example, the expression *ad urbem venire* means "to come to the city." The Latin word is equivalent to the preposition "to."

In his book *Ancient Writing and Its Influences* (New York, 1932), Berthold Louis Ullman locates the origin of the at sign in the sixth century. During the Middle Ages, it was used on religious, diplomatic, and commercial documents to indicate the recipient's name.

Also known as the "commercial at," the @ appeared on typewriters in the 1920s and was then adopted by the telnet network in the 1970s. In 1972, the programmer Ray Tomlinson used it as a word separator for e-mail addresses.

B

CHILDHOOD ROUNDNESS
LIPS

*Second letter of the alphabet
& first consonant*

ORIGIN & EVOLUTION

The second letter of the Proto-Sinaitic alphabet depicts the floor plan of a house. After successive changes to this image the Phoenician BETH developed. Written 𐤁, it is the first letter of the word *bayit*, meaning "house" in Hebrew. This root can still be found today in French words derived from the verb *bâtir* ("to build"): *bâtisse*, *bâtiment*, etc.

The same sign ⌐| existed in Egyptian hieroglyphs, representing a shelter made of reeds. It transcribed the sound of an aspirated [h]. Interestingly, this sound has the same connotation of building in several Indo-European languages: *home*, *house*, *haus*, and *habitation*.

The [b] sound, meanwhile, was represented by the single-consonant hieroglyph representing a foot ⌐.

The transition from Phoenician to Greek, in other words from BETH to BETA, consisted essentially of closing off the bottom half of the Semitic sign: 𐤁 > 𐌁. A second factor contributing to the current form was the reversal of the direction for writing and reading, which was fixed as moving from left to right over the course of the sixth century BCE. From that period on, the letter adopted the shape of our current B.

The Etruscans, reading from right to left, wrote it 𐌁. Strangely, even though this letter appears in the alphabets regularly inscribed on various Etruscan objects—vases, cups, tombstones—it was never used in the body of an Etruscan text.

From a phonetic point of view, B is a voiced bilabial plosive. It is the softest of the labials, approaching P, V, and PH (pronounced [f]).

BAYTOU, the second letter of the Proto-Sinaitic alphabet.

The Phoenician and Hebraic BETH. The latter had a numeric value of 2.

CAROLINGIAN MINUSCULE. The ascender was formed with two overlapping strokes.

In fifth-century RUSTICA, the B, F, and L are slightly taller than other letters.

To the left, GOTHIC FRAKTUR, sixteenth and seventeenth centuries. To the right, two ascender forms from HUMANISTIC CURSIVE, sixteenth century.

The structure of the capital letter.

B

The first Arabic numerals often resembled our modern letters. This is the number 8 from the twelfth century, called *temenias*.

Modern rendition.

SHAPES & INTERPRETATIONS

The letter, in its capital form, is composed of one circle on top of another. Depending on the period, the diameters of these circles were identical or noticeably different, with the smaller circle resting upon the larger, like a snowman. The two bowls are held on the left by the stem. Some see the numeral 13 in the shape of the B, with the stem corresponding to the numeral 1 and the two bowls to the numeral 3.

Its form also evokes the shape of lips, and in various Romance languages the word for mouth starts with B: *bouche, boca, bocca*, all derived from the Latin *bucca*. The letter is also found at the beginning of words that imply use of the mouth, such as the French words *boire* (drink), *balbutier* (babble), *bredouiller* (mutter), *bafouiller* (mumble), *bégayer* (stutter), *baiser* (kiss).

The letter also suggests the roundness of feminine forms. Evoking softness and suppleness, it refers to the world of childhood in words such as *baby, ball, bubble, balloon, babble* (similar to the German term *babbeln*).

Just as the ALEPH symbolized force and unity in the shape of a bull, the BETH leaves us on an earthly plane (in the layout of a house), where we are confronted with the dichotomies of good and evil, life and death. The bipartite structure of the uppercase letter and its numeric value (equal to two) also reveal a sense of duality.

ber

Example of connected letters (be).

-800	0	200	500	800	1200
Greek alphabet	Roman Capital		Rustica	Carolingian	Insular Majuscule	Gothic Textura
	Etruscan	Roman Cursive		Artificial Uncial	Runic-style Insular	Tourneure

THE LETTER IN BRIEF, ABBREVIATIONS & MEANINGS

→ In French printing terminology, in the abbreviation b.d.c. the b traditionally stands for *bas* (below) to designate *bas de casse* (lowercase). Lowercase letters were more frequently used than uppercase letters and were placed into the lower half of the type case (the divided trays into which letters were arranged) in order to make them easier to use.

→ In Anglo-Saxon and Germanic musical notation, where notes are represented by letters, a B corresponds to the Romance si-flat in Germany and to si in England.

→ Followed by three points [B∴], the letter becomes the Masonic abbreviation for *Boaz* or *Booz*. Referring to the left column of Solomon's temple, it maintains a feminine, passive value. It corresponds to mercury and the color black.

→ In French numismatics, a B means that the coin was minted in Rouen; an encircled B, that it came from Brussels[1]; and a doubled B, or BB, that it came from Strasbourg.[2]

→ The abbreviation B.A. stands for Bachelor of Art.

EXPRESSIONS

— The lowercase letter is found in the expression *bdpq, eadem non eadem* (bdpq, the same not the same), which was used to refer to unsteady people and lunatics. As anecdote suggests, this phrase was based on the graphic reversal of the letters. Today, it could be translated as "to change one's stripes" or "to flip-flop."

— A B-movie is a low-budget or low-quality film.

The abbreviation *bus* and the word *fratribus*.

[1] The mark of the Brussels mint in 1939.

BB

[2] The mark of the Strasbourg mint from 1788 to 1834.

Modern rendition of the uppercase.

1400	1450	1500
— Rotunda —	— Batarde —	Chancellery script
— Fraktur —	Humanist	— Modern forms —

C

OPENNESS COSMOS CIRCLE

*Third letter of the alphabet &
second consonant*

The different hieroglyphs pronounced similarly to C.

The Phoenician GIMEL.

The Hebraic GIMEL, representing the number 3.

The four other forms of the archaic GAMMA:
Athens and Argos: ᐸ and ᑕ
Corinth and Euboea: ᐱ and ∧

ORIGIN & EVOLUTION

In Egypt, there were several hieroglyphs with a phonetic value similar to our letter C, keeping in mind its various possible pronunciations.

The first, representing a cup, marks the phoneme [k]. The second shows a water basin and corresponds to the sound [ch]. The last two represent folded cloth and a lock, and are pronounced [s-z]. You may also find the image of a sandy hill indicating the sound [q] or a jar shape ♗ transcribing the guttural [g] sound.

The C is derived from the third letter of the Proto-Sinaitic and Phoenician alphabets. Bearing the name GIMEL, this is the ancestor of the Greek GAMMA with the lowercase shape γ, and the uppercase Γ.

The letter GIMEL is the first initial of the Hebrew word *gamal*, meaning camel. One of the leading hypotheses explaining the letter's origin and evolution was that the original pictogram ⅂, which seems to represent either the animal's hump or neck, became straightened out over time and switched direction toward the right Γ, giving rise to the Greek GAMMA. Today, that thesis is being pushed aside in favor of newer interpretations. Some scholars, for example, note a similarity between the shape of the GIMEL, comparable

400	700	800		1400
Greek	Latin	Uncial		Insular Majuscule	Tourneure	Textura Sine Pedibus
Etruscan	Rustica		Merovingian	Carolingian		Gothic Textura

to the shape of the numeral 7, and the image of a javelin or boomerang, thus implying the idea of movement. Others interpret it as a sort of spike meant for catching fish. The latter theory has the advantage of establishing a link between this letter and the following, the DALETH (△), considered to represent the head of a fish.

The Etruscan letter), derived from the Greek GAMMA, came with some nuances in the notation of the [k] sound. λ [k] was used before a letter A,) [k] before E or I, and ⸰ [q] before a U. Etruscans used another sign to represent the hard C sound [kh], which was written Υ or Ψ. As with the ୫, the letter ⎮ (ancestor of the)) appears in their alphabet but is not used in texts. In the earliest examples of Latin, the C and G were often interchangeable, and the letter C was used to note either the sound [k] or [g].

We should note the similarity in the shape of the upper-case and lowercase C. The form has remained practically the same throughout time. In English spelling the letter C can represent an [s] sound in addition to [k] (*city, circle* vs. *clock*). Together with H it is often pronounced [tsh] (*church*).

SHAPES & INTERPRETATIONS

The shape of the letter C is inscribed in a circle. This incomplete circle remains open on the right side, symbolically toward what is to come, expressing the possibility of leaving a closed-in space. It is the image of a hatching egg, from which a newborn being can escape in order to discover the world. Thus, after staying in the house represented by BETH, the living breath and creative energy contained in ALEPH are liberated toward the exterior.

The classical GAMMA in lowercase and uppercase. The Greek letter had the same numeric value as the Hebraic GIMEL, 3.

IRISH SEMI-UNCIAL, circa 800.

Ligatures for *ct*, Gothic, italic, and typographic.

Modern rendition.

——— Batardes and Cursives ———

— Gothic Rotunda —   — Gothic Cursive —

Fraktur   Modern form

Chancellery

With a comma underneath, the character is called a *cedilla* (from Spanish). In French it is known as a "c with a tail," and it has a softer pronunciation, similar to an S.

To create an optical alignment, the letter extends slightly beyond the x-height on top and bottom.

An abbreviation for *Gaia*, originally written *Caia*. Part of the Roman wedding vows: *Ubi tu Gaius, ego Gaia* (Where you are Gaius, I am Gaia).

The letter C, as the first letter of *caput*.

The image also corresponds to an open mouth. We can think of a newborn, crying at birth for nourishment. This interpretation is echoed in the letters that follow: the D, seen as a door (the exit of the birth canal); the E and F evoking breath (lungs filling with air); and the G representing the complete autonomy of the human race. This last idea may in fact explain the interchangeability of the letters C and G. On a medieval chart of correspondences between Hebraic, Greek, and Latin characters established by the English monk Bryhtferth in 1011 (see p. 28), we find that the letter C is associated with the word *plenitudo*, referring to humanity's complete development. This is similar to the original interpretation of the C as a throwing stick or fishing spike, eliciting the notion of a distance to be covered or a goal to be reached. This same notion is associated with the letter G.

THE LETTER IN BRIEF, ABBREVIATIONS & MEANINGS

→ In the Roman numeration system, C represents 100. With a horizontal bar above it (*titulus*), its value equals 100,000. CC stands for 200, CD for 400, and CM for 900. (The letters D and M represent 500 and 1000, respectively.) In the sixteenth and seventeenth centuries, 1000 was expressed with the sign CIϽ, which resembles the shape of an uncial M.

→ In Roman tribunals, when condemning a criminal, the judges inscribed a C on a tablet, which was then placed into an urn. C was the first letter of the word *condemno*, or "I condemn." This is why the letter was called *littera tristis* (letter of sadness).

→ In Medieval texts, the C appears as the first letter of the word *caput* (head). Usually written as a TOURNEURE letter, traced in red or blue, it marked the beginning of a new paragraph (see glossary, Paraph).

→ In chemistry, a C once represented saltpeter. Today, it represents carbon.

→ The C can be found in ancient treatises on jurisprudence and pharmacy, where it is an abbreviation for the word *codex* (book, with *codices* as the plural).

- → In antiphonaries, a C marks passages that require an accelerated movement, undoubtedly as an abbreviation of the Latin word *currendo*, which comes from the verb *currere* (to run).
- → In Anglo-Saxon and Germanic musical notation, C corresponds to the note DO, formerly called UT. In terms of its vibrations, the U sound, sung on the key of C, acts upon the first *chakra*. Situated at the base of the spinal column (on level with the perineum), this *chakra* controls nervous, circulatory, and sexual functions. It is associated with the color red and connects us to Earth's energies (see U).
- → In mathematics, C represents the set of complex numbers, written ℂ.
- → In the formula, $E = mc^2$, the letter c is short for *celeritas* (velocity).
- → In education C marks an average grade.

The C with a *titulus* was an abbreviation for *cum* (with).

The copyright symbol. This denotes an author or editor's exclusive right to utilize an artistic or literary work for a certain length of time.

D

PASSAGE BECOMING

Fourth letter of the alphabet &
third consonant

The Hebraic letter DALETH, with
a numeric value of 4.

The Greek letter DELTA. Among
the Greeks, it also had a value
of 4.

Abbreviations for *dominus*
(owner, head of the house).

The same word in GOTHIC
TEXTURA, with a ligatured d and o.

ORIGIN & EVOLUTION

Three Egyptian hieroglyphs had a phonetic value similar to
the [d] sound. The first, ➤, represents a hand and was
pronounced [d] or [t]. The second glyph, ◖, resembling
a loaf of bread, had the same pronunciation. The third,
↰, shows a cobra and was pronounced [dsh] as in the
word *journey*.

The letter D has its origins in the Phoenician letter
DALETH, written △. It is the first letter of the Hebrew
words *delet, dad,* and *dag,* which mean, respectively: "door,"
"breast," and "fish." Its triangular or breast-like shape suggests femininity.

Moving into the Greek alphabet, the Semitic DALETH
became DELTA, which in its uppercase form was written as
a triangle pointing upward. The Etruscans, whose writing
moved from right to left, wrote the letter 𝐝 in their alphabet. Oddly, they did not use this letter when writing texts.

The letters D and T (two dental consonants) have
often been confused: in Latin texts, you frequently find the
word *dremere* for *tremere, dremor* for *tremor* (to tremble,
trembling), *at* for *ad, set* for *sed* (but), *haut* for *haud* (not).
The confusion of these two letters is still heard today in
words such as *pied-à-terre* (of French origin), with the D

400	500	700		800		1100	1400	
Roman Capital	Rustica		Uncial	Insular Majuscule		Capital	Gothic Textura	
	Imperial Rescriptums	Ravenna		Luxeuil	Carolingian		Tourneure	Engraved Tourneure

being pronounced [t], or in the soft American pronunciation of the letter T when located between vowels, as in the words *later*, *better*, *greater*, etc.

SHAPES & INTERPRETATIONS

In the Latin world the letter has three primary shapes: D, d, or ꝺ . In UNCIAL script the D returned to the lowercase Greek DELTA structure (δ). This is also true for TEXTURA in the fourteenth and fifteenth centuries, although the letter here became quadrangular.

Among the many shapes of the lowercase d, those of sixteenth-century CURSIVE GOTHIC and BATARDE stand out. The letter can also take many forms within a single typeface, as in ROTUNDA or FRAKTUR.[I]

The musical note D (RE in the notation of Romance countries) is associated with the second *chakra*, which is known by the names *hara* and *tan dien*. Situated two fingers above the belly button, this point is particularly important because it radiates out to the rest of the *chakras*. When we breathe into our stomachs, something we do naturally during sleep, we recharge this point with energy, from where the energy spreads out throughout the body. It is therefore not surprising that the *hara* corresponds precisely to the spot where a child develops within its mother. It is intimately tied to the color orange and the element water (in religious and poetic texts from ancient India, orange is considered the internal color of water).

Abbreviations for the words *significandum* and *notandum*.

[I] Above, the three d shapes in FRAKTUR and two versions in ROTUNDA. Below, the words *die* and *den* in FRAKTUR.

The ligature de. GOTHIC CURSIVE, circa 1530.

The word *garder* in GOTHIC CURSIVE.

In the eighteenth century, the d has a curved shape in BATARDE, FLOWING, and ROUND scripts.

1500

Gothic ———— Gothic Cursive ————

———— Batarde ————

Humanist Round

———— Humanist Cursive —

Modern forms

Character used during the sixteenth and seventeenth centuries for the number 500.

The word *jadis*, with an abbreviated *dis*, in GOTHIC CURSIVE.

Modern rendition of the uppercase.

TOURNEURE letter and a modern rendition of the lowercase in CHANCELLERY.

Abbreviation for *in deo* (in God).

THE LETTER IN BRIEF, ABBREVIATIONS & MEANINGS

→ The Semitic DALETH and the Greek DELTA share the numeric value of 4. Whereas the number 3, associated with the triangle, represents the spirit, the number 4 is associated with the square and represents matter. It brings us closer to terrestrial reality (the four cardinal points, the four elements, the four seasons).

→ In one of the notation systems adopted by the Greeks for writing numbers with letters, DELTA was worth 10. Based on the principle of acrophony, letters corresponded to numbers that begin with that initial: so for example, DELTA and DEKA (ten). Δελτα > Δεκα = 10.

→ In Roman numerals, the D has a value of 500. Here, the D is the right half of an uncial M.[2]

→ Topped with a *titulus*, the D indicates 5000, and with a double *titulus* 50,000. CD = 400.

→ In mathematics, D stands for the set of decimal numbers.

→ In ancient medical prescriptions, d appears twice in the code *d.d.vitr.*, for *detur de vitro*, or "give in a glass."

→ In chemistry, D stands for vitriol, the former name for ferrous sulfate or copper sulfate. This was used for mixing metallogallic inks, for which the other main ingredient is the tannin extracted from gall nuts.

→ In U.S. politics, D often stands for Democrat.

→ In economics, D abbreviates *demand*.

E

BREATHING HOPE
TRANSPARENCY

*Fifth letter of the alphabet
& second vowel*

ORIGIN & EVOLUTION

The Egyptian hieroglyph representing a reed or double reed[1] is associated phonetically with the Latin vowels E and I.

The origin of our E dates back to the Phoenician letter HE, which was formed from the Proto-Sinaitic sign HE representing a man with his arms raised to the sky.[2]

Depending on the time period, the direction of reading and writing changed, and the letter HE's evolution followed the mechanistic modifications and reversals this change brought with it. The sign adopted by the Greeks, called EPSILON, was definitively turned to the right in the sixth century BCE. The Etruscans, who wrote from right to left, wrote it ꓱ. Turned again toward the right, the uppercase letter came to the Latin world and western European notation in the form E. The shape of the lowercase is generally quite different than the uppercase.

E is the letter that occurs most frequently in written English. In English spelling it can represent many different vowel sounds, illustrated by the words *debt, scene, serpent, fallen, new,* and *the.* The sound that comes closest to the Latin quality of [e] is the vowel in *bed,* while the name of the letter, "E" [ee], is pronounced more like the Latin letter I. A final silent e often signals that the preceding vowel is long (*rate* vs. *rat*).

SHAPES & INTERPRETATIONS

The shape of the Proto-Sinaitic HE, a man with arms raised upward, recalls an attitude of prayer or invocation. In this context, it is interesting to note that the Semitic HE is used twice in forming the divine tetragrammaton *Yod He Vav He,* designating the name of God. Today, the letter's shape no longer bears this divine connotation. Turned on the horizontal,

[1] Egyptian glyphs resembling a reed or double reed.

[2] The Proto-Sinaitic HE.

The Hebraic letter HE has a numeric value of 5.

Archaic Greek forms, circa 700 BCE.

ε E

The Greek EPSILON, equivalent to the number 5.

Unique letter shape in GOTHIC CURSIVE, circa 1520.

INSULAR-style ampersand, early ninth century.

Anglo-Saxon abbreviation for the Latin pronoun *eius* (of him/ of her).

LUXEUIL MINUSCULE: the ligatures *ex* and *ec* and the word *saeculi* (generations).

Ligatures for *est* in LUXEUIL MINUSCULE and INSULAR MAJUSCULE.

Abbreviation for *est* (is) and three abbreviations for *esse* (be).

Abbreviation for *id est* (that is).

it seems to indicate the interest that humans have for others, for their own kind. However, through its various graphic and phonetic uses, it still maintains the notions of respiration and breath inherent to its shape.

The letter is present twice in the name Eve, and in the French language many masculine adjectives become feminine with the addition of a final e (*un–une, premier–première, absent–absente*).

A lowercase e was often joined to the letter that followed it by extension of its median bar. You can clearly see this in Carolingian texts where it connects to most other letters:

ea	ef	ei	em	en	es	et

The E, pronounced [eh, ay] and sung on the musical note G, stimulates the fifth *chakra*. This is located on level with the throat and is associated with the color blue (a feminine color), with the sky, and with notions of coolness and respiration. The E, airy, light, and almost immaterial, may be related to ether, air, breath, or spirit. In his poem entitled "Vowels," Rimbaud associates it with white, a symbol of purity and the sum of all the colors in the rainbow.

With the E, we also enter into the dynamic symbolism of the number 5, with its connection to the human body, clearly illustrated by Leonardo da Vinci's drawings. We may also think of the five fingers on the hand or of the five senses.

"tertio"

100	400		700		800	1000	1400
Roman Capital	Rustica		Uncial			Cursive	Textura Sine Pedibus
	De Bellis	Quadrata		Artificial Uncial	Carolingian	Textura	Gothic

Insular Majuscule

THE LETTER IN BRIEF, ABBREVIATIONS & MEANINGS

→ An E with a cedilla, as found in Carolingian manuscripts, is the equivalent of the contracted æ.[3]

→ In chemistry, an e once stood for etherine. Today, it is used in physics as a symbol for an electron.

→ The uppercase E corresponds to energy: $E = mc^2$.

→ On a compass, map, or weather vane, E stands for East.

→ In early European prayer books, E stood for Thursday, with A standing for Sunday.

→ For the Romans, E had a value of 250, as this Latin verse shows: *E quoque ducentos et quinquaginta tenebit.* Topped with a *titulus*, it had a value of 250,000.

→ In colloquial English, E can stand for the synthetic drug Ecstasy.

→ In Anglo-Saxon musical notation, E corresponds to the MI of Romance countries, the note that vibrates through the third *chakra*. Located at the solar plexus, it has a natural correspondence with the color yellow.

→ The symbol for European currency is based on an UNCIAL-shaped E.[4] We may assume that the double line used in this currency will soon be replaced by a single line, as was the case with the U.S. dollar and the sterling pound.

3 Abbreviation for æ; the cedilla is the bowl of the a.

The word *habet* in INSULAR MINUSCULE.

Mathematical symbols. The first means "there exists"; the second and third show inclusion in a set or exclusion from a set.

e-mail e-book

The e stands for "electronic."

4

1500

| Tourneure | English Batarde | | Tourneure | | Engraved Tourneure | | Italic | |
| Rotunda | | Batarde | | Gothic Cursive | | Gothic Fraktur | | Modern forms |

The ligature *nt*, shown in *habitant*.

Abbreviations for *etiam* (also), *et hoc* (and this), and *et sic* (and so).

AMPERSAND

The ampersand is expressed typographically as &, formed by the graphic contraction of e and t—representing the conjunction *et* (Latin for "and"). In CAROLINGIAN MINUSCULE, the ligature appeared as &, where the letter t is completely inverted or upside down. The copyists who reproduced this sign were unaware of the inverted orientation of the t, which was also found at the end of certain words.

The t quickly regained its normal orientation, thanks to scribes who enlarged the upper right-hand part of the ampersand, assuming that this was the bar on the t, when in fact it was the serif. Most modern et ligatures reproduce the "upright t," except the symbol & where it remains inverted, as at its origin. This symbol has acquired international recognition, preserving its meaning throughout the world.

During the eighth century, it evolved as follows:

| CAROLINGIAN | ——— GOTHIC ——— | ITALIC |

The POETICA font offers a wide array of ampersand forms. Here are a few of them:

F

**BREATH DANGER
MASCULINITY**

*Sixth letter of the alphabet
& fourth consonant*

ORIGIN & EVOLUTION

In Egypt, the [f] sound was represented by the hieroglyph ⌒, shaped like a horned snake. The origin of our letter F dates back to the sixth letter of the Proto-Sinaitic alphabet, called WAW. It was written either —o or ⌐, signs that represented an oar, a peg or hook, or a sled. The Phoenicians took up the vertical form of the Proto-Sinaitic WAW and opened its upper portion (Y). The shape of their sixth letter, also known as WAW, led to several interpretations: it could be a headrest (still used in Africa), a phallus, or an oarlock (a metal or wood piece used to hold a boat's oars).

Two Greek letters were formed from the Phoenician WAW: the consonant DIGAMMA ⊢ which stood for the [w] sound and the vowel UPSILON, Y in its classical version, pronounced like the German ü [y]. The first, which is the basis for our F, owes its shape to the fact that, in passing from Phoenician to Greek, the upper part of the letter was rotated to the left. This rotation can be seen in archaic Greek alphabets (from the seventh and eighth centuries BCE). There, the letter comes in various forms depending on the region of origin; it was written ⌐ or ⌐ in Crete and ⌐ in Boeotia.

The second letter derived from WAW, Y, closer to the letter's original structure, appears in the following forms in archaic Greek: Y Y Y V. It gave rise to the letters U, as well as V and W in the Latin alphabet (see U).

The letter DIGAMMA is composed of two overlapping GAMMAS, hence its name. It disappeared quickly from Greek alphabets but was reintroduced by the Etruscans to transcribe the same sound, either [v] or [w]. To indicate an [f] sound, the Etruscans originally placed a letter H next to the DIGAMMA, creating the digraph FH, written ⊢目.

The Hebraic WAW, with a numeric value of six.

The Phoenician WAW, thirteenth century BCE.

The letter DIGAMMA in archaic Greek. It was numerically equivalent to the number 6.

Etruscan forms, the first shapes to mark the [f] sound, around 650 BCE.

The Etruscan DIGAMMA transcribed a [v] sound.

In RUSTICA, the F is taller than other letters, much like the B and L. This elongated form was used quite rarely.

The word *deffendre* (to defend) in GOTHIC CURSIVE, 1530.

Later, they wrote this sound using a sign resembling an 8.[I] An F was added to the Latin alphabet during the first century BCE, at the same time as the letters Y and Z.

As we saw above, the F and V are connected historically. This interweaving can be found in the etymological evolution of the word *brief* from medieval French *bref* from Latin *brevis*. The close connection of the two sounds is also found in words such as *wife/wives, knife/knives, thief/thieves*, where the spelling and pronunciation changes from F to V in the plural. Etymologically, this is explained by a phonological rule in Old English, according to which F remained voiceless at the beginning and end of a word but became voiced when occurring between vowels. (The E vowel in the plural of these words was originally prono unced.)

SHAPES & INTERPRETATIONS

The meaning attributed to the Hebraic letter WAW may support a phallic interpretation. Besides being the coordinating conjunction *and*, it also indicates the masculine gender in Hebrew. In fact, there is an inherent principle of juncture and linkage in this letter, so in terms of bodily symbolism, the WAW may also be related to the spinal column, which connects the head to the rest of the body (and more specifically to the lungs). As the phallus, it weaves a connection, binding the lover to the beloved. In addition, the Hebrew word *waw* (written with two WAWs) means "nail," "ankle," or "hook," which by extension implies the terms "pipe," "canal," "spinal column," and "phallus."

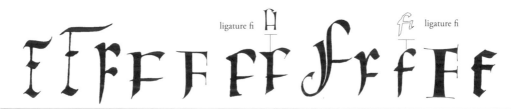

ligature fi   ligature fi

	500		700		800	1100	1300
Rustica		— Uncials —		— Insular Majuscule and Minuscule —		Tourneure	
	Rustica, Paraph		Artificial Uncial			Carolingian	Textura

In CAROLINGIAN MINUSCULE, an f is differentiated from a "long s" with a bar at the height of the shorter lowercase characters. This allowed for ligatures with any letters that followed. In the typographic ligature fi, the dot above the i is indistinguishable from the droplet-shaped tip of the f.[2]

As a sound, the letter evokes the breathiness of words such as *feather*, *fly*, and *sniff*. In addition, in words such as *fresh*, *frigid*, *fridge*, and *frosty* the letter F followed by an R vibrates and conjures an image of cold.

In the words *fraud*, *perfidious*, *false*, and *fickle*, the F sound approaches the [s] sound (like a serpent), evoking danger and trickery.

THE LETTER IN BRIEF, ABBREVIATIONS & MEANINGS

→ In the Roman world, an F represented the number 40; topped with a *titulus*, it indicated 40,000.

→ As the first letter of the word *fugitivus* (fugitive), F was used to mark slaves who had tried to escape. Later, the letters T.F. (*travaux forcés*) were branded on French criminals who were condemned to hard labor. It was only in 1832 that this practice was abolished.

→ F abbreviates the Latin term *fecit* (made it), which was often added by painters after their name when signing a canvas.

→ In chemistry, the letter F on its own used to represent iron. Today it is written "Fe."

→ °F stands for "degrees Fahrenheit."

ponnficer fidem

The words *pontifices* (pontif rulers) and *fidem* (faith, trust) in CAROLINGIAN MINUSCULE.

The ligature *fi* in STEMPEL GARAMOND ROMAN.

The ligature *fe* in GOTHIC TEXTURA.

Abbreviation for *folio* with a superscript O.

ligature ff   ligature fi   variants

1400		1500	
Textura	Rotunda	Fraktur	Chancellery
Textura Sine Pedibus	Batarde Majuscule and Minuscule	Humanist Round	Modern forms

ff fff

In music, ff and fff stand for *fortissimo* (very strongly).

→ Sung on the note F of Anglo-Saxon and Germanic musical scales (FA in Romance countries), the vowel A releases its vibrations into the fourth *chakra*, located on level with the heart and lungs (see A).

→ In physics, F is the abbreviation for farad (for Michael Faraday), a unit that measures electrical capacitance.

→ In the colloquial expression *F-word*, the initial stands for the word *fuck*.

→ In photography the f-stop indicates how open the aperture of the camera lens is (f from focal length).

EXPANSION GERMINATION GRANDEUR

Seventh letter of the alphabet & fifth consonant

ORIGIN & EVOLUTION

In Egypt, there were four hieroglyphs with a phonetic value close to G. The first shows the outline of a jar ◖ ; the second represents a basket with a handle ➤ [k]; the third resembles a sandy hill ◢ [q]; and the last glyph, a cobra at rest ➘ [dj].

The letter G is an indirect result of the Phoenician GIMEL and the Greek GAMMA, both of which are the basis for our letter C. The G appeared relatively late in the Latin alphabet, and its creation is attributed to Appius Claudius. In 312 BCE he fashioned this new letter from the letter C in order to distinguish the consonant's softer pronunciation (at the time, C was pronounced in the same way as our K). Some scholars maintain, however, that the G was not introduced into the Latin alphabet until around 250 BCE.

It was placed in the seventh position of the alphabet, where the Phoenician ZAYIN or the Greek ZETA stood. This position was available for the G because Latin speakers had no need for a Z to write their language. They removed that letter from their alphabet, only to reintroduce it during the first century CE in order to transcribe words of foreign origin. In order not to shake up the alphabet, the Z was then placed at its very end.

The G is a soft guttural consonant. In English spelling the letter represents a voiced velar plosive in words such as *get* or *bag*; an affricate as in *gin*, *edge*; and a velar nasal in words such as *ring*, *sing*. In terms of its pronunciation, the G is close to the Greek GAMMA and the Hebraic GIMEL (see C), both of which are positioned third in their alphabets.

In French, a D has often been substituted for a Latin G, such as in *fingere*, which became *feindre* (to feign), or *pungere*, which became *poindre* (to come up). Many words that have since been simplified once bore a "final g," such as

The Hebraic letter GIMEL, with a numeric value of 3.

G

The Athenian form, sixth century BCE.

ANTIΛENE

The name ANTIGENE. Antigenes's tomb, Athens, circa 500 BCE.

A monogram composed of a GAMMA and RHO, abbreviating the Greek word *graphetai* (is written), ninth century. Sometimes written into the margins of manuscripts, it referred readers to other texts.

Rare forms in UNCIAL and INSULAR scripts.

Modern forms.

6 ɡ

RUSTICA, fifth century.
The first example is based on a
spiral; the second was mostly
used in footnotes.

RUNIC-style uppercase.

The word *generibus* in IRISH
SEMI-UNCIAL, around 800.

The letter g and the ligature *gi* in
intellegit, LUXEUIL, seventh and
eighth centuries.

besoing, today *besoin*, or *loing*, today *loin*. The verbal forms
of these words still bear the trace of that lost letter: *besogner*,
éloigner, etc. In English there is a similar simplification in
the silent pronunciation of the G before N in words such as
feign or *sign* (Latin *signum*). There is also a permutation of
the letters G and W between Romance, Anglo-Saxon, and
Germanic languages. For example, the German verb *warten*
(to wait), and the English verb *to ward* correspond to the
French *garder* (a word that in turn comes from the Frankish
wardôn, "to watch over or be on guard"). Similarly, the German verb *wachen* (to keep watch) corresponds to the French
guetter, and the noun *Wache* to *guard*, the English word here
derived from the French *garder*.

We can also cite the French word *gateau* (cake), derived
from the Frankish *wastil* (food); the verb *to guide* from the
Frankish *witan*, meaning "to show a direction"; and, finally
Wilhelm and William, which became Guillemus in Latin
and Guillaume in French.

SHAPES & INTERPRETATIONS
EVOLUTION OF SHAPE IN THE LOWERCASE

In ROMAN and IRISH SEMI-UNCIAL, as well as in ANGLO-SAXON
MINUSCULE, the g is written as a horizontal line connected
below to a kind of cedilla with a loop that is more or less
opened. Because of this, it often resembles a z or the numeral
3. Starting in the sixth century, in ROMAN SEMI-UNCIAL
script, the left end of the upper bar curved gently (ƺ).
That tendency became accentuated in MEROVINGIAN script
(of the LUXEUIL variety) whose g also had an upper loop

ligature gy

500	600	800	1150	1500
Rustica	Merovingian	Insular Minuscule	Gothic Primitive and Textura	
— Uncials —	Irish Semi-Uncial	Carolingian		

that was completely closed. The great cursivity of that script generated some rather remarkable ligatures. Those that combined the g with another letter deserve notice for their interesting shapes. Here are a few of them:

| ga | ge | gi | gm | gu |

The CAROLINGIAN g borrowed from this form. It is easily ligatured with most other letters by extension of its ear.[1]

Since the earliest times, the spiral that is the basis of the uppercase G has been a symbol of life, growth, and fruitfulness. Its shape recalls movement and revolution. The G fittingly is the first letter of the prefix *gyro-* (from the Greek *guros,* "circular movement," "circle").

There is an element of vitality in the letter G, a symbol of birth (the *grain* from medieval French *grain/graine,* from the Latin *granum/grana*). This is evident in words such as *germinate, gamete, genesis.* It also points to terrestrial reality as in the prefix *geo-* or the Greek terms *Ge* and *Gaia,* designating the Earth.

As a guttural consonant, the G is associated with the throat and with speech (*guttural* from medieval French *gutturale,* from Latin *guttur,* "throat"). It is also associated with eating (*glutton, gourmet, gastronomy*), and is found in many words that imply grandeur: *grand, great, grandiose, gigantic* (and the prefix *giga-*), *grandiloquent.* François Rabelais himself named his giant hero Gargantua.

The ligature *gn* in CAROLINGIAN MINUSCULE.

[1] POETICA CHANCERY I, DEMOCRATICA REGULAR, and STEMPEL GARAMOND 35-point. These examples demonstrate different loops and ears.

G G G

The design of certain majuscules evokes a counter-clockwise motion.

35-point FETTE FRAKTUR.

Modern rendition.

variants

1500

Gothic Fraktur

Modern forms

Gothic Batarde

Chancellery

In the Middle Ages, a G indicated 400. With a *titulus* (Ḡ), it stood for 400,000. Some scholars claim it had a value of 3, like its ancestor, the Greek GAMMA. With a *titulus*, it would then correspond to 3,000.

Gammut

This word is based on the Greek letter GAMMA. It was first used in the eleventh century by Guido d'Arezzo as a name for the first note of the octave, then for the whole octave, known at that time as "gamma-ut."

The abbreviation for *gent* in the French word *d'argent*. GOTHIC CURSIVE, fifteenth century.

THE LETTER IN BRIEF, ABBREVIATIONS & MEANINGS

→ Engraved on first-century Italian monuments, G is often the first letter of the name *Gaius* and the following words: *Galliae* (the Galls), *Gallicus* (Gallic), *Germania* (Germania), *Gratus* (in gratitude).

→ In chemistry, the letter G corresponded to glucinium. Today, this is better known as beryllium (Be), a solid, light metal often used in alloy fabrication.

→ In physics, g represents the force of gravity, which varies with altitude and latitude. Body weight is defined by the formula $P = mg$, where m represents mass.

→ The uppercase letter abbreviates the prefix *giga-*. This multiplies the unit it precedes by 10^9.

→ As a unit of weight, the letter g corresponds to the gram.

→ In Anglo-Saxon and Germanic musical notation, the G corresponds to the SOL of Romance countries.

→ In freemasonry, the letter G has special significance. Most often, it is found in the center of a five-pointed star, known as the flamboyant star. Here, it implies glory, generosity, grandeur, genius, generation, gnosis (knowledge), gravitation, geometry. Derived from the Greek GAMMA with its squared shape, the letter G indirectly recalls the right angle and consequently connotes objectivity, rigor, and force.

→ A film rated G by the Motion Picture Association of America is suitable for a general audience.

H

STABILITY CONSTRUCTION
COLUMNS

*Eighth letter of the alphabet
& sixth consonant*

ORIGIN & EVOLUTION

There are several Egyptian hieroglyphs that transcribe the [h] sound, with varying degrees of aspiration. One represents a courtyard in a house or a shelter made of reeds. It is pronounced like the H in the verb *to have*. Another sign shows the image of a rope made of woven flax and is pronounced like the H in the name *Hamed*. A third represents a cow's udder or its stomach and tail and is pronounced more softly, as in the German *ich*.

Our letter H is derived from the Phoenician HETH and the Greek HETA. Its pictographic shape, III, symbolizes various forms of borders: a wall, a fence, a field, or an enclosure. Its evolution is relatively simple. First, it was pivoted 90 degrees, representing more of a ladder shape 目, and subsequently a domino 日. This evolution ended in classical Greek with only one rung remaining on the ladder: **H**.

In terms of its phonetics, the Phoenician letter HETH was a guttural, comparable to ALEPH. In the crossover to Greek, it was integrated as the HETA consonant, transcribing the [h] sound. It also became the vowel ETA, with a softer pronunciation corresponding to a [long e] in Ionian Greek. This vowel/consonant ambivalence is still evident in French nineteenth-century dictionaries, where a fair amount

These three hieroglyphs correspond to the [h] sound.

The Hebraic letter HETH. Its numeric value is 9.

From the Phoenician HETH to the archaic Latin H.

The Etruscan form, from a tablet from Marsiliana d'Albegna.

ligature ho

FIRST CENTURY	500	600		800	900	1000
Roman Capital	Rustica		Luxeuil Minuscule	Carolingian Minuscule		Beneventaine
De Bellis		— Uncial —	— Insular Majuscule —		Gothic Script	

CAROLINGIAN form.

The number 5 in the twelfth century. It was also called *quimas*.

The H is the first letter of many words denoting shelter: habitation, home, *habit* (Fr.), *Haus* (G.), hamlet, house, hut. It is also an initial indicating elevation or height: *hieros* ("sacred," Greek), *hagios* ("holy," Greek), helium (lighter than air), *helios* ("sun," Greek), height, head, and *haupt* (" head," German), hoist, hoopoe, hero.

(1)   (2)   (3)

(1) Ahiram, thirteenth century BCE
(2) Seventh century BCE
(3) Eshmunazar, fifth century BCE

of space is dedicated to explaining the pronunciation of the French H. With the first pronunciation, called *H aspirée*, H was considered a consonant since "it adds a guttural force to the vowel that follows." With the second pronunciation, called *H muet*, it was considered a vowel. In general, the H in Romance languages is not pronounced, and through medieval French the silent H was also introduced into the English language (compare the silent pronunciation of *honest* to the aspiration of *hat*).

At the time of Clovis (fifth century), the Franks used the letter H to mark heavy aspirations: *Hlothaire* became *Chlothaire*, then *Clotaire*.

SHAPES & INTERPRETATIONS

The first shapes the HETH borrowed coincided with the Hebraic sense of the word *heth*, which means "border" or "fence." This was no longer true once the sign was turned 90 degrees and became the image of a ladder.

The number of ladder rungs changed over time, often according to location. Between the thirteenth and fifth centuries BCE, the Phoenicians wrote the letter with two, three, or four crossbars. Later, the Greeks wrote it with three at first, then only one. There were either three or four in Etruscan writing, and in archaic Latin, the H was still written with the shape 𝐁.

By switching from horizontal to vertical, the sign no longer presented the image of an obstacle but one of potential elevation. It became the ladder that unites Heaven to Earth.

ch

1200   1400

Textus Quadratus ——— Gothic Rotunda ———   Gothic Cursive

——— Textura Majuscules ———   Textura Sine Pedibus

Batarde

The word *human* seems to affirm this idea: humans, who are humble (from the Latin *humulis*, "low, near the ground"), aspire to ascend to the heavens. Thus, the letter H symbolically represents a stage in human life.

There are also several points in common between the letters H and B (see B). In Egypt, these two letters shared the same hieroglyphic representation: ⊓. As we mentioned above, one of the hieroglyphs for the [h] sound resembled a shelter made of reeds or the courtyard of a house. The two letters in fact seem to play a determining role in words relative to construction: *inhabit, build, hamlet.*

The H and B each have a bipartite structure in the uppercase, and a nearly identical shape in the lowercase (b, h). This is especially true in CAROLINGIAN MINUSCULE (ƀ, ƀ). The shape of the capital letter imparts great stability. The crossbar connecting the two stems effectively reinforces the overall structure. This is a noble letter, made in the image of a temple.

Even though the lowercase, with its chair-like silhouette, is different from the uppercase, both share a sense of stability and groundedness. Similarly, the H marks a phonetic elevation of the accompanying letter, particularly when used in onomatopoeias:

MMMH! Ah, Ah, Ah! Ooooh!

In the fifth century, a few curves were introduced into the uppercase shapes. The H's right stem bows toward the right in RUSTICA. It has a wider shoulder in UNCIAL.

The word *honore* in INSULAR MINUSCULE, circa 800.

GOTHIC MAJUSCULE, circa 1500.

RUSTICA and UNCIAL from the fifth century.

1500

Fraktur Majuscules —— Engraved H —— Chancellery script ——

Fraktur Minuscules   Humanist Round   —— Modern forms ——

H-S H-L-S

The two first initials stand for *sestertium* (large sesterce); the second three, *sestercius* (small sesterce). These Roman coins were made of silver and brass.

Road sign. The letter here stands for "hospital."

THE LETTER IN BRIEF, ABBREVIATIONS & MEANINGS

→ During the Middle Ages, an H had a numeric value of 200. Topped with a *titulus*, it was worth 200,000.

→ In chemistry, the H represents hydrogen (H_2O). In physics, it is the symbol for henry, a unit for measuring electric inductance.

→ Both in the uppercase and lowercase, the letter abbreviates the word *hour* (km/h, H hour), as well as the terms *height* (h or ht) and *hospital* (H). It can also represent heroin.

→ In German musical notation, the letter H corresponds to B natural.

→ In academia an honorary degree is indicated by h.c., which abbreviates *honoris causa* (for the sake of honor).

→ The abbreviation ha stands for hectar.

I & J

VERTICALITY ELEVATION
JOY CLARITY

Ninth letter of the alphabet & third vowel (I)
Tenth letter of the alphabet & seventh consonant (J)

ORIGIN & EVOLUTION

In the Egyptian hieroglyphic alphabet, the two signs that were pronounced similarly to the Latin vowel I (pronounced as the English i, ee, y, ie, as in *sit, see, city, brief*) represented a blossoming reed or pair of reeds, the latter sometimes appearing in a more stylized form: \\. Some scholars think that the I evolved from the hieroglyph ▬, representing a forearm and hand. It appears, however, that that symbol corresponds to the Semitic consonant AYIN, conventionally written as ᶜ and pronounced [ᶜâ]. Nevertheless, the Proto-Sinaitic pictogram is also shaped like a forearm and hand. Over time it was turned several times and ended up as ↑, the sign the Phoenicians used to transcribe the YODH, ⟨, from which our I derives.

The Hebraic YODH, with a numeric value of 10, is the first letter of the word *yad*. In Hebrew, this means "hand," which explains the connection established with the hieroglyph mentioned above. The value of YODH also equals the number of fingers on two joined hands (as if in prayer). This union of hands represents exchange and the balance of opposing electromagnetic forces (the fingers on the left hand producing an "inverse" energy charge from those on the right hand).

In the Medieval chart of correspondence between Latin, Greek, and Hebraic letters (see p. 28), the word *principium* (beginning, foundation, origin), is associated with the letter YODH (written *Ioth*). Perhaps this association reflects the fact that YODH is the first letter of the divine tetragrammaton *Yod He Waw He.*

Unlike other Hebraic signs, this letter floats above the writing line and is shaped like a sprouted seed. This special positioning makes it the only sign that is not connected to the Earth.

Egyptian hieroglyphs
The reed, double reed, and the stylized form.

The Hebraic letter YODH.

The Phoenician YODH, circa 825 BCE.

The Phoenician YODH as it appears on the tomb of King Ahiram, thirteenth century BCE.

The Creation of Adam by Michelangelo, Sistine Chapel. Through his index finger, God gives life to Man. In *La langue hébraïque restituée*, published in 1815, Antoine Fabre d'Olivet writes that the YODH represents the human hand, the index finger.

The i topped with a diacritic mark in 1323 and 1400.

The abbreviation for *us* in the word *ejus*, genitive form of *is, ea, id* (he, she, it, this, that).

Abbreviations for *ei* (in the word *dei*) and *in* (in the word *inter*), CAROLINGIAN MINUSCULE.

i !

The shape of the letter i resembles a human silhouette. Upside down, it is an exclamation point, used in texts to express intense emotion. It is also found in road signs to warn drivers of upcoming dangers.

The YODH became the IOTA when it passed into the Greek alphabet. There, it is represented by a simple stem, except in eastern Greek, where it was written ⟨, similarly to the letter SIGMA. This shape, however, disappeared quickly.

The Etruscans didn't differentiate between the E (a very closed vowel) and the I. In Latin, the letter I was used both to write the consonant J (pronounced as the Y in English *yes*) and the vowel I. In addition, on a number of documents, the long form of the letter I, called *littera longa* (long letter), replaced ii and ei. We find *DIs* for *Diis* (Pluto, god of the underworld) and *otI* for *otii* (leisures).

In modern English the I represents mainly a short [i] as in *sit* and the diphthong [ai] as in *mine*, which is due to the Great Vowel Shift of the fifteenth century, when the Middle English long [i] changed to [ai].

SHAPES & INTERPRETATIONS

In terms of shape, the I is the simplest of signs, reduced to a single vertical line (see Straight Line, phallic symbol). Symbolically, it unites Heaven and Earth. As a microcosm of the human body, it represents the spinal column, uniting the head and feet. The [i] sound lends a "sharp" quality to words such as *strict, stringent, shrill, acid*.

There has not always been a dot above the letter. In fact, it was not until the eleventh century that the dot appeared, as a prolongation of the stem's upper part. This helped make the letter more distinct, since it was often confused with m, n, and u. The dot was still used rarely at that time, and a century passed before it entered into general use.

Long form

100 500		700 800		1000	1200		1500	
Roman	Uncial	Carolingian	Beneventaine					Batarde
Rustica		Gothic Primitive		Textura				
	Irish Semi-uncial							

Besides the dot, the letter is also topped in French with a circumflex accent, î, or an umlaut, ï, as visible in the word *naïve*, borrowed from the French.

According to the *Dictionnaire des symboles* (Éditions Bouquins), "the I evokes brilliance, lyricism, the illusory, becoming, rhythm." Rimbaud connected the letter to the color red. In my opinion, it also has a correspondence with the color yellow and its simple geometric equivalent: a triangle pointing upward. That shape is a symbol for the spiritual world (see A). It is often represented with an eye in its center or the four letters of God's name: *Yod He Waw He*.[1]

THE LETTER IN BRIEF, ABBREVIATIONS & MEANINGS

→ Its vibrating nature: when sung on the musical note A, the [i] sound (pronounced as in *see*) acts upon the sixth *chakra*, known as the "frontal *chakra*," and in India as *ajna*. Located between the eyebrows, this point is also called the "third eye" or the "eye of wisdom." It is associated with the rather appeasing color indigo, a dark blue tinged with violet.

→ In inscriptions, an I is most often short for *Iesus* (as in "INRI"),[2] *Imperator* (leader), *Iovi* (to Jupiter) or *Iulius* (Julius). The three letters *IHS* (or *JHS*) form the abbreviation for *Iesus* (or *Jesus*) *Hominum Salvator*: Jesus, Savior of Men. They are also the first three letters of the Greek word ΙΗΣΟΥΣ (*Iesous*).

→ As the first letter of the word *intercedo*, the I was sometimes engraved on wax tablets used by Roman tribunals

Ioseph

The name *Ioseph* (Joseph) in CAROLINGIAN MINUSCULE.

[1] The numeric value of YODH, 10, reduces to unity (symbol of the divine) when the digits 1 and 0 are added.

INRI

[2] The abbreviation for *Iesus Nazarenus Rex Iudaeorum* (Jesus of Nazareth, King of the Jews).

— Humanist —   Letter of civility

— Fraktur —   — Chancellery script —   — Modern forms —

ISBN

The abbreviation for International Standard Book Number. An ISBN, used to identify books, is composed of thirteen digits. The ISSN (the standard for magazines) is made up of eight digits.

The abbreviation for *unus* (one) or *primus* (first).

The abbreviation for *quatuor* (fourth). In order to avoid confusion, numbers were often placed between dots.

[ʒaʁdɛ̃]

[xɔta]

[ˈdʒuːliət]

The phonetic transcription of the French word *jardin* (garden), the Spanish *jota* (a folk dance), and the English name *Juliet*.

3 Louis Meigret, *Traité touchant le commun usage de l'escriture*, 1542.

for voting. This meant a vote for suspending one of the Senate decrees.

→ I is the chemical symbol for iodine. As a lowercase letter, it is a symbol in physics for the intensity of an electrical current (measured in amperes).

→ Today, an I placed in a circle means "information."

I, AS NUMERIC LETTER IN ANTIQUITY

The Greeks used the tenth letter of their alphabet, the IOTA, to indicate the number 10. In contrast, in ancient Rome, an I represented one unit, and became 1,000 when a dash (*titulus*) was placed over it. In that same system, an I indicated a subtraction of 1 from the number to its right, (IV = 4, IX = 9, IC = 99), or the addition of 1 to any number on its left (VI = 6, XI = 11, CI = 101, MI = 1,001).

As we have seen above, the long I (*littera longa*) had a double phonetic value. The numeric letter I also had a long form, similar to a J, which was used to mark the last unit in a number terminating in 2, 3, or 4. This helped to avoid any errors in interpreting a series of numbers that seemed identical. As such, you find VIJ for 7 or XIIIJ for 14. This method of writing the final I longer than the letters preceding it appeared in the fourteenth century. Roman numerals, which were considered more difficult to falsify than their Arabic counterparts, remained in use in the financial world for a long time.

THE LETTER J

Toward the middle of the sixteenth century, the letter J, also called the "consonant I," was forever split from the I. Until then, the two letters had often been interchanged. This new scission was due to the influence of the humanist, poet, and mathematician Jacques Peletier (1550) and of the humanist, mathematician, and philosopher Petrus Ramus or Pierre de la Ramée (1557). A few years earlier, in 1542, the grammarian Louis Meigret had already suggested separating these two letters as representing different sounds.[3]

The first printers to use the two letters distinctly were Dutch, which is why the J was called an "I from Holland" in the profession for many years.

In English, the letter represents a voiced palatal-alveolar affricate. The Italians have never added the J to their alphabet. They use a G to indicate a similar sound to the English J in words such as *giorno* (day) and *giardino* (garden). The Spanish give the letter a strong guttural aspiration, represented by the phonetic symbol [x]. In French, the letter J, pronounced [ʒ] has often replaced what was a G in Latin, for example in the words: *jumeaux* (twins), from *Gemini*, *jambe* (leg), from *gamba*, and *joie* (joy), from *gaudium*.

ABBREVIATIONS

—J∴ corresponds to the Masonic abbreviation for Jakin, the name given to the right-hand pillar of Solomon's temple. Associated with the color red, it symbolizes activity and masculinity.

—In physics, J is short for joule.

—In colloquial use, J can stand for the word *joint*.

The Proto-Sinaitic sign.

From left to right, the Hebraic letter KAPH, followed by a FINAL KAPH. The eleventh letter of the Hebrew alphabet, KAPH has a numeric value of 20. The FINAL KAPH is equivalent to 500.

-830   -800   -450
Phoenician forms.

K κ κ

Fifth-century RUSTICA and rare forms from the tenth century.

K

POWER FORCE EARTH

Eleventh letter of the alphabet
& eighth consonant

ORIGIN & EVOLUTION

Two uniliteral Egyptian glyphs had a phonetic value close to [k]: ◢ ◥. The first represents a sandy hill, the second a cup or basket with a handle. In the Proto-Sinaitic alphabet, the image of a hand 🖐 represented the letter KAPPU, pronounced [k]. This origin is supported by the fact that in Hebrew, KAPH (the name given to the letter), means "palm of the hand," "sole of the foot," or "hollow." After being simplified, the Proto-Sinaitic sign became the eleventh letter of the Phoenician alphabet: the KAPH (or KAF), written ⊬, which is found as 7 in Armenian.

Adopted by the Greeks, who wrote from left to right starting in 550 BCE, the letter was turned to the right and given the name KAPPA (κ, K).

To represent the [k] sound, the Etruscans used three different signs: K (written ⋊) was only used before an A sound; C (written ⟩) before an E or I; and Q (written ⚲) before a U sound. At the very end of their alphabet, the Ψ sign stood for a [kh] sound.

When the Romans invented the letter G to record a sound that was softer than C, the latter took on a harder pronunciation, causing a near disappearance of the letter

ᛕ K ᛕ K ᛕ k k ᛕ K k Ҡ k

300		700	800	1300		
Quadrata		Insular Minuscule	Carolingian Minuscule	Tourneure		Textura
	Uncials	Luxeuil Minuscule	Gothic Primitive	Rotunda		

K

k k k

Above, three variations of
CAROLINGIAN MINUSCULE, ninth
century. Left, modern forms.

85

K

K. In fact, when Greek words were adopted into Latin, the
KAPPA was converted to C.

The letter K appeared only rarely in texts from the
Middle Ages, essentially as an initial for the words *Kæso* (for
the first name *Cæso*), *kalendae* (the first day of each month),
or *Karolus* (*Carolus*, Charles). It was only toward the end of
the twelfth century, with the arrival of texts edited in ver-
nacular languages, that the letter was used more regularly.
Romance languages today still use K only in words that were
derived from other language groups (Slavic or Germanic).
The Celtic languages also used C to mark a [k] sound, which
influenced Old English spelling. Today English is the only
Germanic language that uses the letter C in addition to K to
transcribe a hard [k] sound (*clock, common, compare*).

The abbreviation for the Latin
term *kalendas* (calends, the
first day of the month), around
1200. The expression *ad kalendas
Græcas* (at the Greek calends)
means "never," since Greeks did
not have calends.

1500

Textura

Fraktur

Batarde

Charlemagne's monogram, composed of the letters in *Karolus*.

Sumerian pictogram; pronounced [ku], it meant "to eat." Related to the Earth.

[1] Sumerian pictogram, used for the word "mountain," pronounced [kur], circa 3300 BCE.

SHAPES & INTERPRETATIONS

The word *kaph* means "the palm of the hand." More generally, it imparts the idea of a cup or receptacle. The relation of the consonant [k] to the hand is visible in words that borrow the Greek prefix χειρο (*chiro-*) such as χειρομαντεια (chiromancy, palm reading), *chiropractor*, or *chirography*. These three words place importance on the hand, with the first word making particular allusion to the palm. Like the soles of the feet, each palm is a *chakra* point. These so-called minor *chakras* are in addition to the seven main ones listed on page 41. More precisely, the right hand releases any extra electromagnetic charge from the body, whereas the left receives a charge from the surrounding environment. This distinction of each hand is well understood by whirling dervishes who dance with the left hand pointing to the Earth and the right to Heaven.

Only the Sumerian word *kur*[1], which means "mountain," seems to capture the full essence of the letter K, expressing power, force, solidity, and hardness, both in terms of its pronunciation (as an unvoiced velar, occlusive consonant) and its graphic depiction. Similarly, the Greek word το κερατο (*keras, keratos,* "horn") expresses the notion of hardness and duration. This root is also found in the word *corn* (as on a toe, from the Latin *cornu,* "horn, point"). In a more modern register, the word *rock* evokes the same idea.

The letter K is also connected with an earthly notion and with matter. The Greek word κακος (*kakos,* "bad") gives us the Latin word *cacare* (to shit), found in the German word *kacken* or the French *caca*. Yet the consonant also expresses

Humanist script

Chancellery

Letter of civility

Modern forms

grandeur and force, as in the word *colossus*, derived from the Greek *kolossos*. It is also the first letter of the words *ka* and *ki*: The first is a term in Egyptian religion that represents all of the vital energies animating gods and men. The second, which is also written *qi* and *chi*, is well known to those who practice martial arts or study Chinese medicine. It means breath or energy.

In the Middle Ages, the shape of the lowercase k was close to that of a t, to the point that it was possible to confuse the two letters. Over the course of time, there has been little variation in the shape of the lowercase, which is based on the uppercase form. Its structure was only modified in certain GOTHIC scripts.[2]

THE LETTER IN BRIEF, ABBREVIATIONS & MEANINGS

→ The numeric value of the letter K is 150 or 250. With a *titulus* above it, it stands for 150,000 or 250,000.

→ In information technology, K multiplies the number preceding it by 1024, or 2^{10}.

→ The uppercase letter K used to indicate degrees in Kelvin. Absolute zero is equivalent to 0 K, or -459.67° F.

→ In chemistry, K stands for potassium. It is the first letter of its former name: *kalium*.

→ A lowercase k is the abbreviation for kilo. It multiplies the unit following it by 1000 (km/kilometer).

2 WITTENBERGER FRAKTUR, 30-point. The K, of Germanic origin, is characterized by its shortened, horizontal lower branch.

The letter K lends power to the following words:

khan, of Persian origin, Mongol ruler or Tartar chieftain.
Krach, German for "noise."
Kraft, German for "force, power."
krak, from the Arabic *karat* (fortress).
kremlin, from Russian. *Kreml* means "fortress."
ksar, from the Arabis *qsar*, a fortified village.
kyrie, from the Greek *Kurie* (Lord).

^I Egyptian hieroglyphs.

The Hebraic LAMEDH.

Phoenician forms.

Etruscan form (read from right to left), around 700 BCE.

CAROLINGIAN form. Notice the thicker top of the stem. It was formed with two strokes, an upstroke and a downstroke.

L

LIQUID SQUARE SOFTNESS

Twelfth letter of the alphabet & ninth consonant

ORIGIN & EVOLUTION

The two Egyptian hieroglyphs^I associated phonetically with the letter L represent a lion and a mouth. They may also be pronounced [r].

In the Proto-Sinaitic alphabet, the letter that is the basis for our L looks like a staff: ⟂. After being simplified, it was written ⎰ by the Phoenicians, resembling a raised arm. Placed in the twelfth position in their alphabet, it bears the name LAMEDH, a Hebrew word that means "goad," or "staff." From the twelfth to the fifth century BCE, it maintained this form. As the staff served to poke and direct animals, this shape imparted a notion of discipline, instruction, and education.

The Greeks borrowed the Phoenician LAMEDH and renamed it LAMBDA. Its shape and direction were variable at first (⎰⎰⎰) but ended with the classical form Λ. In Argos as well as in Athens, this was the way the GAMMA was written (they wrote the LAMBDA as V and, more rarely, as ⊢). Starting in the second century BCE, the letter was used as a numeric sign, which had the same value as the Hebraic LAMEDH, 30. While the direction of writing was ultimately fixed from left to right in the Hellenic world, the Etruscans

ıſıťl abbreviation

Ļ

ЦиLıLıLЄLıLLıLıLııı

	450		500	700	800			1100		1300		
Rustica			Artificial Uncial	Insular Majuscule				Carolingian		Tourneure		
	Roman Uncial			Merovingian		Insular Minuscule			Gothic Primitive			Textura

wrote in the opposite direction. This led to another rotation of the letter **V**, becoming **√** in northern Italy in the seventh century BCE.

The L often became a U in words passing from Latin to French, such as *paume* from *palma* or *haut* from *altus*. In English spelling some words include a silent L (*talk, calf, half, could*), which was once pronounced in Old English. In other words, such as *palm*, the silent L was deliberately reintroduced to refer to the word's Latin origin. In fact, the French word *paume* was borrowed during the Norman occupation, so the L of *palm* was never pronounced.

SHAPES & INTERPRETATIONS

In ROMAN CAPITAL script, a character's balance was dependent on its proportions of height and width. The most aesthetic proportion was close to 1.5 (see golden number, p. 36). As with the Greek GAMMA, the L was shaped like a square, its right angle symbolizing rigor, instruction, and rectitude.

In its lowercase form, the letter is generally written as a simple vertical line. This not only leads to confusion with a capital I, but can complicate reading as in the word *Illegible*.

In GOTHIC TEXTURA or FRAKTUR the L sometimes has an added spur, which is connected to the stem at the height of the shorter lowercase letters.[2]

The letter's phonetic structure is one of roundness. Soft, light, and liquid, it is found in words such as *liquid*, *float*, *flow*, *lap*, *fluid*, *lick*, and *lull* as well as in the names of the

The crossed l, besides being the initial for *libro* or *liber* (book), was used in several types of abbreviations. Abbreviations "by suspension" consist of only the first part of a word; the suppression of the final letters is indicated with an appropriate sign. For example, *tal* with a crossed l was used for *talis* (such):

In *multo* (a lot) and *plura* (more), it represents an elision with a u:

The capital letter is inscribed inside an upright rectangle, with dimensions proportionate to Φ, or 1.618.

The ligature *Lu* in TOURNEURE letters.

The character used by the Etruscans for the number 50.

The sterling pound symbol. Currently written as above, it was originally crossed by two bars, as was the American dollar sign. The double bar is still found on currencies such as the yen (¥) and, more recently, the euro (€).

Modern form.

angels Gabriel, Daniel, Raphael, and Uriel, the bearers of strength, justice, medicine, and divine light, respectively. In the word *alleluia*, the letter L amplifies the vowel sounds.

THE LETTER IN BRIEF, ABBREVIATIONS & MEANINGS

→ In the Roman world, L had a numeric value of 50. With a *titulus* above it, it became 50,000.

→ The letters L.S. appear on certain medieval diplomas as an abbreviation for *locus sigilli*, which means "place of the seals." In more recent times, the literary abbreviation l.c. signifies *loco citato* (passage cited).

→ On ancient Greek medals, a LAMBDA (Λ) was written in its archaic form ∨, which was its shape in Corinth and on the isle of Euboea. It is an abbreviation of the word ΛΥΚΑΒΑΣ, which meant "year" in ancient Greek.

→ With a crown above it, the letter referred to the French kings Louis XII, Louis XIV, or Louis XV.

→ A symbol composed of two interlaced L's also stood for Louis.

→ The letter abbreviates liter. It was also the former chemical symbol for lithium, today written Li. A pound is abbreviated lb (from the Roman term *libra*, "scales, balances," which was also a unit of measurement).

→ In mathematics L or l stands for the length of a line.

→ In ancient Rome L was the abbreviation for the first name Lucius.

M

AQUATIC VIBRATING HUMAN

Thirteenth letter of the alphabet & tenth consonant

ORIGIN & EVOLUTION

Two Egyptian hieroglyphs are associated with the letter M through their pronunciation, the first representing an owl, the second a gazelle rib. It is, however, by its form that the unilateral hieroglyph 〰, shaped like waves and pronounced [n], is related to the M. In the Proto-Sinaitic alphabet, our letter M's ancestor was in fact written ᴟᴟᴟ. The Phoenicians rotated the character vertically, leading to the shape ᶎ (in the Ahiram form). M is the first letter of the Hebrew word *mem*, which means "water." Its original shape, evoking the Egyptian sign, shows a stream of water or ocean waves, signifying a current or a river.

In Aramaic, at the end of the eighth century BCE, the letter underwent a first transformation, changing from vertical to horizontal ᶎ > ᴟ. The second stage of its transformation is characterized by a simplification of the "small waves" design, as well as a variation in the number of waves. Its definitive form was attained in the Greek MU (M). The Etruscans wrote it ᴟ, similar to the Ionian Greeks (in the form of the Greek alphabet Milet). Nevertheless, it passed into Latin and Western alphabets shaped like the classical MU. Its current form still maintains a sense of its original meaning: water.

The Hebraic letters MEM and FINAL MEM, indicating 40 and 600, respectively.

91

M

The two hieroglyphs pronounced [m].

(1) (2) (3)

The Phoenician MEM: (1) as it appears on the tomb of King Ahiram, thirteenth century BCE; (2) on the Mesha Stele, an inscription by a Moabite King, ninth century BCE; and (3) on the tomb of Eshmunazar, King of Sidon (present-day Saida), fifth century BCE.

μ M

The Greek letter MU stood for the number 40.

The Etruscan letter in its archaic form, followed by two third-century (BCE) forms.

A rather remarkable version discovered in Pompeii graffiti. This sign consists of four vertical lines, the first longer than the other three.

An exceptional form in IRISH SEMI-UNCIAL, circa 800.

Imago leonis, in RUNIC MAJUSCULES.

In its cursive forms, the M reverts to its original shape. GOTHIC CURSIVE, 1523.

In terms of phonetics, the M is a bilabial nasal consonant, in other words, to pronounce it, both lips are used and air is sent into the nasal cavity.

SHAPES & INTERPRETATIONS

There is an aquatic motion inherent to the letter M, represented by the image of flowing water. Through its association with water, the M may be considered the most human of letters, embodying maternal liquidity. It is therefore natural to find it in words such as *man, woman,* and the terms for *mother* in various languages: *mère, maman, madre, Mutter.* As one of the easiest consonants to pronounce, it is among the earliest sounds babies make around the world.

What's more, the mere pronunciation of the letter, the vocalized [em] sound (which is considered a vowel in India), causes a vibration in the most compact region of the human body: the brain. This explains its usage in the Indian mantra for relaxation [om] or [aum], acting upon the seventh *chakra* at the crown of the head. When sung on a B^b, the [om] sound resonates with the colors violet, white, and gold.

In China, the practice of *koto-dama,* which means "spirit of sounds," was used to influence people spiritually, physically, and mentally. Each sound has a particular signification: the [mu] corresponds, for example, to the phenomenon of birth and maternity; the [mo] represents harmony, roundness, and the mother; and the [mi] is connected to the "me." In the onomatopoeia *mmmh,* expressing pleasure, we find a perfect illustration of the underlying positivity of the letter's vibratory nature.

Associated with the water element, the M is symbolically at the source of all material life, and through its sound

1300   1400   1500

Textura Sine Pedibus   Gothic Batarde

Textura Majuscule   Rotunda

and physical sensation, it is at the source of all spiritual life. In its double aspect, the M seems to realize the perfect union of body and soul. It takes its natural place at the heart of our alphabet, in position thirteen.

THE LETTER IN BRIEF, ABBREVIATIONS & MEANINGS

→ For the Romans, an M equaled 1,000.[1] With a *titulus*, which multiplies a number by one thousand, $\overline{M}$ corresponds to 1,000,000.

→ M. is the abbreviation for *Monsieur*. Doubling the letter as MM. denotes the plural *Messieurs*. Mr. is the abbreviation for *Mister*.

→ As a lowercase letter, it abbreviates the following terms: *masculine*, *meter*, *mega-*, and *milli-*.

→ M.A. corresponds to the expression *Magister Artium* (Master of Arts).

→ The letter is also a symbol for the Holy Trinity, due to the three triangles in its form.

→ H.R.M. is short for "His/Her Royal Majesty."

→ According to the principle of duality in the Hebrew tradition, *mi* and *ma* represent the waters of Genesis. The theological *mi* (pronounced [me]) designates the waters "from on high" and the anthropological *ma* represents the waters "from on low." The vowels I and A indicate the "spatial position" of the M based on their higher- and lower-pitched sounds (ascending and descending).

→ Military weapons, such as guns and tanks, often have an M in front of a number to identify them (M16 rifle, M2 Bradley combat vehicle, M9 Beretta); the M stands for *model*.

[1] Originally, the Romans wrote the number 1,000 as ∞, M, or ꟿ. One half of that last symbol was used for 500, written Ɔ or as a letter D.

Another way of writing M as a number corresponding to 1,000, sixteenth and seventeenth centuries.

The number 1,000, between the eleventh and fourteenth centuries. The *titulus* replaces the M.

Superscript M. The French word *commençant* (beginning) in GOTHIC CURSIVE.

LUXEUIL MINUSCULE, seventh and eighth centuries. The elongated shape of the final M in the particle *eum*.

1500

Gothic   Chancellery

Gothic Cursive   Humanist Round   Modern forms

N

INTERIORITY NEGATION BIRTH

Fourteenth letter of the alphabet & eleventh consonant

The FINAL NUN appears in the word *nun*, meaning "fish" (reading from left to right).

The Proto-Sinaitic NUN.

The Greek NU, like the Hebraic NUN, has a numeric value of 50. The FINAL NUN has a value of 700.

The Phoenician NUN.

On the left, a late form of the Etruscan N, during the fourth to first century BCE; on the right, a rare form similar to the M, written ⊞ at the time.

ORIGIN & EVOLUTION

The two hieroglyphs ⌇⌇⌇⌇ and 𓏥 are uniliteral characters from the Egyptian alphabet that transcribe the [n] sound. The first represents flowing water, the second a red crown. In the Proto-Sinaitic alphabet, this same phoneme is denoted by a snake image, which was then taken up by the Phoenicians, who accentuated the curve of the line and simplified the shape by removing the snake's head, resulting in the sign ラ, the fourteenth letter of their alphabet, the NUN. The Hebraic letter derived from it bears the same name, which in Aramaic means "fish" or "water snake." In terms of its shape, our N is derived from the Greek NU, itself a result of the Phoenician NUN. The first Hellenic inscriptions present the letter NU with the form ⅂. This is also found in archaic Etruscan inscriptions from the seventh to fifth centuries BCE, and in the first Roman writings such as the Lapis Niger. By making the letter vertical and balancing out the stems, we arrive at its current shape, already in use in classical Greek from the fifth century BCE.

The uppercase form was only slightly altered over time, except in twelfth- and thirteenth-century diplomatic documents, where the letter's shape matches that of the H.

0	500		700	
Pompeian graffiti	Roman Uncial		Artificial Uncial	Insular Minuscule
	Rustica	——— Uncial ———	—— Insular Majuscule ——	

Once it appeared in the cursive scripts of the sixth century, the lowercase n looked like our modern letter. Thicker and more stable in CAROLINGIAN MINUSCULE, it maintained a similar frame in the centuries that follow, modified only slightly by the various subsequent styles.

In the GOTHIC CURSIVE scripts of the fifteenth and sixteenth centuries, a lowercase u could be differentiated from an n only by context.[1] The two letters were both constructed on identical vertical or angled stems.

SHAPES & INTERPRETATIONS

The letter N is associated with the notion of birth, demonstrated by the prefix *neo-*. In 1815, the writer Antoine Fabre d'Olivet in *La langue hébraïque restituée* expounded on this connection by writing of the NUN that "as a symbolic image, it represents the son of Man, every individual being produced." The Hebraic letter represented great qualities, such as purity and power, which had to be hidden from view in order to remain intact.

In the table established by the English monk Bryhtferth in 1011 (see p. 28), the word *sempiternum* (eternal) is related to the N. As we saw above, the letter's origin connected it to fish, the animal that in Christian iconography is associated with Christ.[2]

The letter's link with the water element is also found in the Greek word *nero* (το νερο), "water." In Etruscan, this was *neri*, whose root is visible in words such as *navigate, nautical, navy, naval*, etc. Indispensable to life, water is intimately linked to sexuality, well-being, and ease (like a fish in

ν N

The Greek letter NU, lowercase and uppercase.

punctum

[1] The word *punctum* (point) in GOTHIC CURSIVE, circa 1530.

ROMAN SEMI-UNCIAL, fifth century.

UNCIAL ligatures for NS, NT, and NC.

ο ιχθυς

[2] The Greek word *ichthus* (fish), composed of: *Iesous CHristos THeou Uios Soter* (Jesus Christ, Son of God, Savior).

nn nn n nn N Nn N N nnn

800	1170		1400	
Carolingian		Tourneure		Textura Sine Pedibus
Roman Semi-uncial	Gothic Primitive		Gothic Textura	— Gothic Batarde —

Italic majuscules and minuscules from the sixteenth century.

The word *omnibus*, derived from *omnis* (all). The letter N is replaced by a *titulus*, and the *us*, by a semicolon.

Abbreviation for the word *domino* (lord), INSULAR MAJUSCULE.

ñ

Abbreviation for the word *non* (not), end of the twelfth century.

n̄c n̄d

Abbreviations for the words *nunc* (now) and *nondum* (not yet).

water). It reminds us of our own origins, those that precede our coming into the world (our nascence), when we were still floating in the maternal womb.

Returning to the letter itself: in the first century CE, the Roman rhetorician Quintilian (Marcus Fabius Quintilianus) called it the *littera tinniens* (the chiming letter), remarking on the fact that its sound is clearer and franker than other consonants.

In CAROLINGIAN MINUSCULE, the n resembles the arch of a bridge or a rounded Romanesque vault. Its Gothic form was also shaped like an arch, but a ribbed or broken one.

Except in Greek, where ναι [nai] means "yes," the letter N expresses negation in numerous languages (*no, ni, non, nein, nyet*). Its pronunciation creates a vibration in the face (as a nasal letter), which can be described as reassuring, internal, appeasing, tender, and intimate.

Just like the M, the letter N often appears in manuscripts as a fine horizontal line, called a *titulus*, which is placed above another letter, most often above E and U. The *titulus* is found in words such as *legēs* for *legens* or *ignorāt* for *ignorant* (from fifteenth- and sixteenth-century Latin manuscripts and texts).

THE LETTER IN BRIEF, ABBREVIATIONS & MEANINGS

→ In the Roman numeral system N had a value of 900. With a *titulus*, it became 900,000.

→ In official Roman acts, N.P. is an abbreviation of *notarius publicus*.

→ On the Roman calendar, N was short for the word *nonus* or *nonis*, the ninth day before the ides, the monthly

1500

Fraktur

Humanist Round

Modern form

Cursive

Chancellery

noſter

division situated either on the thirteenth or fifteenth day of the month.

→ The formula III N. stood for *tertio die ante nonas* (the third day before the *nonus*).

→ The letter often replaced the word *non*. In manuscripts from the Middle Ages, you find the letters NL for *non liquet* (it is not clear).

→ N.B. is the abbreviation for *nota bene* (note well).

→ On compasses, maps, and weather vanes, an N replaces the word *north*.

→ Nº is short for the word *number*. The superscript letter is an O (from Latin *numero*).

→ In mathematics, the letter denotes an unknown power (example: a^n). Similarly, you find its indeterminate value in the expression "for the nth time."

→ In chemistry, N represents nitrogen (once called azote), and in physics, a newton.

→ An N abbreviates the prefix *nano-* (from the Greek *nanos*, "dwarf"). This divides the unit following it by 10^9 (nanosecond, nanometer).

→ In early medical prescriptions, an N stands for *numero*: *Æther. gutt. n. X* for *ætheris guttæ numero decem*, in other words: "ten drops of ether."

→ Its sinuousness, similar to the letter Z, indicates a series of sharp curves on road signs.[3]

→ In colloquial English, 'n' is sometimes used as a substitute for the word *and* ("scratch 'n' sniff").

The letter shape in GOTHIC BATARDE in the word *noster* (our).

The abbreviation for the Latin word *neque* (neither).

The abbreviation for the word *ante* (before).

The abbreviation for the word *enim*, an affirmative adverb that means "for, in fact, indeed."

The mathematical symbol representing the set of all natural numbers.

3 Road sign.

O

ROUNDNESS SOFTNESS
FEMININITY

*Fifteenth letter of the alphabet
& fourth vowel*

The Hebrew word *ayin* means
both "spring" and "eye."

The Hebraic letter AYIN and the
OMICRON each have a numeric
value of 70. The OMEGA, Ω, has
a value of 800.

ORIGIN & EVOLUTION

The two Egyptian hieroglyphs that are most similar to the letter O in terms of pronunciation represent a quail 𓄿 (or its stylized version 𓄿), denoting the sounds [o, u, w], and a noose 𓍢, marking the sound [o].

In the Proto-Sinaitic alphabet, the ancestor of our letter O represents a realistic eye 👁, an image that was later simplified to the form ⬬. This sign, denoting a guttural consonant, was adopted by the Phoenicians in a rounder form without the pupil ° and called AYIN, which means "eye" in Hebrew and is related to fountains (*fons* in Latin) and springs in our medieval table (see p. 28). The marriage of these two ideas (eye + fountain) can be translated as "a teardrop." The Greeks borrowed the Phoenician letter to represent the vowel sound [o] and baptized it OMICRON, or "little O." In certain regions and time periods, the dot reappeared in the center: in Thira (in the southern Cyclades), in Crete, and in ancient inscriptions from the eighth and seventh centuries BCE. At that time, in order to avoid confusion, the THETA was written ⊗ or ⊕. Later, when the OMICRON dropped its dot, the THETA took the shape ⊙.

By opening up the bottom of the OMICRON, the Ionians created the letter OMEGA. This "big O," placed at the end of

300	400	500	700	800	1100	1400
Quadrata		Uncial		Insular	Gothic Primitive	
	Rustica		Luxeuil		Carolingian	Gothic Textura

the alphabet, marked a longer pronunciation of the vowel. The letter's terminal position is recalled in the expression "from alpha to omega," as in the words of Christ: *Ego sum* A *et* ω[1] (I am the alpha and the omega).

The Etruscans borrowed the Greek OMICRON, but it appears only in the alphabets inscribed on various objects and never in their texts, as with the letters B, D, and G. In Etruscan texts, the O shape (with or without a central dot) and the letter ⊗ correspond to the [th, a more emphatic t] sound (see also T). The shape of our O, as the evolution of this letter attests, can be traced directly back to that of the Phoenician AYIN, its ancestor.

In modern English spelling, the letter O can represent many sounds. Think of words such as *bone, clock, foot, glory, some, word*, etc., in each of which the o marks a different sound. The vowels in *glory* and *clock* are closest to the sound quality of the Latin O.

SHAPES & INTERPRETATIONS

Since its inception, the O has been based on a more or less elongated circle. In certain Greek inscriptions of the second century CE, it has more of a diamond shape, a form that reappeared between two bars in the seventh century, in runic-style INSULAR MAJUSCULE.[2] It is rectangular in GOTHIC TEXTURA (in the fourteenth and fifteenth centuries), but

1

εςοsuϾ Ᾱ ᴄᴛ ω

[2] Above, the remarkable layout of the O in the Lindisfarne Gospels, end of the seventh century.

Left, the word *Poleos*, second century CE, with a diamond-shaped OMICRON and a W-shaped OMEGA (connected to a SIGMA).

oc

The conjoined letters o and c, in HUMANIST CURSIVE.

1500

| Gothic Textura | | Gothic Batarde | | | Humanist Round | | | Modern forms | |
| Rotunda | | | | Fraktur | | Chancellery script | | | |

O *O*

Unlike the static first character, called "Roman," the second one, in italics, connotes motion, pulling the letter to the right.

The circle, as a perfect figure, is the symbol of heaven (the square is associated with the Earth). It integrates the notions of time (eternity) and of cycles, implying return. It also evokes the family or, more generally, a group of individuals (roundtable, teepee, places around a fire).

The abbreviations for *agro* and *corpus*. The superscript O replaced *ro* and *or*.

In death records, a crossed O is the abbreviation for the Latin *obitus* (dead). It also represents the Greek THETA, the first letter in Θανατος, *thanatos* (death).

more almond-shaped in other Gothic scripts such as fifteenth-century BATARDE or sixteenth-century FRAKTUR. Its shape recalls a breast, the maternal womb, or an egg (the word *oval* comes from the Latin *ovum*, "egg"). By extension, this letter represents an enclosed and protected world, but one that does not preclude the notion of passing between interior and exterior. Rimbaud connects the vowel to the color blue, so that the letter is related to the feminine world both in its shape and its associated color.

The interjection *O* or *Oh* is used to denote "the various movements of the soul," such as surprise or astonishment. The mouth naturally adopts the letter's shape in order to pronounce it.

In the fourteenth century, Giotto, the Florentine painter and architect, demonstrated his talents before Pope Benedict IX by drawing a perfect circle in a single brushstroke. From then on, the expression "Giotto's O" referred to a perfectly rounded figure.

In early musical scores, the O sign was used to indicate a three-count measure, considered a perfect measure. A halved character, or C, indicated an imperfect two-count measure.

According to the *Dictionnaire des symboles* (Éditions Bouquins), the letter invokes enclosure, death, order, orderliness, loftiness, and inevitability.

THE LETTER IN BRIEF, ABBREVIATIONS & MEANINGS

→ In the Middle Ages, the O had a numeric value of 11. With a *titulus* above it, it became 11,000.

→ The nine antiphonies sung during Advent, during the seven to nine days preceding Christmas, are known by the name O. These accompany the hymn "Magnificat" in which each song begins with an O: "O rex gentium, O Emmanuel."

→ The superscript O (º) appears in the abbreviation for *folio*, written fº. It is also used to denote degrees of temperature in the Celsius or Fahrenheit system: ºC and ºF and for measuring angles as well as latitude (35º N) and longitude (40º E).

→ O.P. stands for *Optimo Principo*, which means "to the very excellent Prince."

→ In chemistry, the letter stands for oxygen. Formerly, it also represented alums or any gold-based alloy. As a doubled letter (OO), it stood for oil.

→ In medicine, O (or o) is one of the human blood types in the ABO blood group system.

→ The lowercase letter is sometimes used as an abbreviated form of *of*, as in *ten o'clock*.

The "short O" sound, sung in the key of D, acts upon the second *chakra* (*hara*), while the "closed O" that can be found in some languages, sung in the key of E, acts upon the solar plexus, the position of the heart *chakra*.

A zoomorphic letter from 1519.

P

SPEECH EARTH PEACE

Sixteenth letter of the alphabet
& twelfth consonant.

The Phoenician form found on
the Yehimilk inscription, circa
950 BCE.

The Hebrew letters PE
(equivalent to 80) and FINAL
PE, with a numeric value of
800.

ORIGIN & EVOLUTION

The Egyptian hieroglyph that was pronounced [p] represents a chair, either as a horizontal or vertical rectangle ▤. For a long time, the hieroglyph ⬭ (representing an open mouth) was incorrectly associated with the letter P. In fact, it was pronounced [r] and sometimes [l], much like the lion-shaped hieroglyph. There probably existed a Proto-Sinaitic letter denoting the phoneme [p], but this has not been established definitively. It may have been the sign ⊔.

While the Egyptian sign ⬭ is thus not related to our P, numerous documents and scholars have shown that the letter does in fact correspond to the mouth and palate. The letter PE (פ) in turn is the initial of the Hebrew word *peh*, which means "mouth." It has been established that our P is derived from the Phoenician PE, written ٦.

The Greeks adopted the Phoenician letter into their alphabet under the name PI. In ancient Greek, it was written ٦ and in Ionian Greek Γ, to eventually become the uppercase Π and lowercase π in classical Greek (the Greek letter with the shape P was called RHO, pronounced [r]).

The Hebraic PE and the Greek PI both correspond to the number 80.

0	400	500		800	1100	
De Bellis	Uncial	Artificial Uncial		Insular Minuscule	Carolingian	Abbreviation for *pro*
	Quadrata	Rustica	— Insular Majuscule —	Merovingian	Capital	Gothic

The Etruscans, reading from right to left, wrote the letter **ꓶ**. Toward the third century BCE, under Latin's influence, the direction was reversed again and the sign was then written **ꓭ**. It was subsequently completely closed: **ꓑ**.

The B and P were often confused due to their relative homophony, so that numerous manuscripts present *optulit* instead of *obtulit*, or *apsens* for *absens*.

SHAPES & INTERPRETATIONS

The most unique shapes occurred during the first centuries CE. For example, in first- and second-century CURSIVES (traced on walls, wax tablets, and papyrus), the second line forming the letter did not have the curved shape that we have come to know today. The P was thus sometimes very difficult to identify.[1]

In first-century DE BELLIS script, the bowl is only slightly curved and does not close onto the stem, which makes the letter resemble a C.[2]

In seventh- and eighth-century MEROVINGIAN script (of the LUXEUIL variety), the stem's form illustrates that the letter was written in a single movement, without lifting the pen from the page.[3]

In GOTHIC TEXTURA, the bowl of the P sometimes serves as the stem for the letter that follows it: pa, pe, po, or pp. In that form, letters are called "conjoined."

In FRAKTUR, the descender of the P sometimes appears merely as a finely traced vertical line, and the letter's bowl can take two possible styles.[4]

1

Remarkable shape found at Pompeii, first century.

chiliccꝟ

[2] The name *Philipp(us)*, as it appears on the sole parchment fragments remaining from the earliest Latin codex. Dating from the first century CE, this document is called *De bellis macedonicis*. There are no serifs, and the letters have unique shapes, like the P above.

[3] The ductus for the letter in MEROVINGIAN MINUSCULE.

[4] The two bowl forms in FRAKTUR and an example of conjoined letters (PP).

1300	1400	1500

Gothic Primitive — Gothic Textura — Gothic Majuscules — Modern forms

Tourneure letter Chancellery script

CHANCELLERY script.

po *pe*

Conjoined letters *po* and *pe*.

SPQR

The abbreviation for *Senatus Populusque Romanus* (the Roman senate and people).

%

This typographical sign for percent contains a ligature imitating handwriting. GRANJON, 24-point.

p

Crossed with a bar through its descender, the letter becomes *per*.

The lowercase p in sixteenth-century CHANCELLERY scripts takes the following shapes:

p p p

The design of the uppercase P differs considerably from letter to letter.

The character's bowl started to open up around the beginning of the seventeenth century in the ENGLISH style and in other scripts of the period, producing these shapes:

Stirling, Barcelona, 1830. De Beaugrand, Paris 1601. Senault, Paris 1670.

THE LETTER IN BRIEF, ABBREVIATIONS & MEANINGS

→ During Roman antiquity, the letter P had a value of 100 (like the letter C) or 400. Topped with a *titulus*, it became 100,000 or 400,000. More rarely, you find P = 700 and $\overline{P}$ = 7,000.

→ In pharmacy, P stands for *pugillium* (pinch) or for *pars* (part).

→ In chemistry, P represents phosphorus.

→ In physics, Pa is the symbol for a Pascal.

→ P. S. is the abbreviation for *post scriptum*, placed at the end of letters.

→ In certain manuscripts, *p. kal.* abbreviates *pridie kalendarum*, the day before a calend (the calend was the first day of the month).

→ A lowercase p. or sometimes pg. is the abbreviation for *page*, and pp for *pages*.

→ In musical scores, p signifies *piano*, pp calls for *più piano* (and sometimes for *pianissimo*), and ppp stands for *pianissimo*.

→ The metric prefix p. corresponds to the unit pico, or 10^{-12}.

→ In typography, pt. stands for point, the smallest unit of typographic measurement.

- → In the Middle Ages, several additional dashes create various meanings for the letter P. You find ꝑ̄ for *propter,*[5] ꝑ for *per* or *par,* and in Old French, ꝓ for the prefix *pro-*.
- → In English the letter is used in the phrase "to mind one's Ps and Qs."
- → In schools P is used as a grade to indicate "passing."

[5] Another abbreviation for *propter* (next to, beside), often used after the tenth century.

p̃ leſpit de ure cuer

Par l'esperit de votre cuer (By the spirit of your heart), Old French on a document dating from 1294.

ABBREVIATING VALUES

p̃　ꝑma　caꝑ　ꝑte　ꝑt　opa

pri　　*p'*　　*caput*　*parte*　*post*　*opera*

A plate of FRAKTUR letters. Van den Velde, 1620.

The Hebraic letter QOPH resembles a hatchet. Its numeric value is 100.

On the Hebrew calendar from Gezer, tenth century BCE.

(1) The Phoenician QOPH from the Yehimilk inscription, tenth century BCE, and (2) on the tomb of King Eshmunazar, fifth century BCE.

The Etruscan letter. On a tablet from Marsiliana d'Albegna, circa 700 BCE.

Q

WISDOM FERTILIZATION HATCHET MONKEY

Seventeenth letter of the alphabet & thirteenth consonant

ORIGIN & EVOLUTION

The hieroglyph ◢ is a uniliteral sign from the Egyptian alphabet. Resembling a sandy slope or hill, it was pronounced [q].

In the Phoenician alphabet, our modern letter's ancestor could be either ∞ or 𐤒, which became 𐤒 (QOPH) in Phoenician and can be interpreted in several ways. It could represent the eye of a needle or a monkey (translated in Hebrew as *qoph*), an animal associated with wisdom. It could also be the image of a double axe. The sign mainly expressed an act of cutting. From a symbolic point of view, this may stand for the individual's acceptance of his own isolation in order to gain wisdom.

The letter's sacred nature is confirmed by its relationship to the Latin word *vocatio*, which means "vocation" or "calling," on the medieval table of correspondences (see p. 28).

Among the Greeks, the character derived from the Phoenician QOPH bears the name QOPPA or GOPPA. This guttural letter, placed between PI and RHO in their alphabet, became obsolete during the sixth century BCE, however, it was conserved as a numeric sign for the number 90. It appears in its archaic form 𐤒 in Thira (Santorini) and Crete, and was

0	400		800	1400
Roman Capital	Quadrata		Uncial	Carolingian Minuscule	— Gothic Textura —
	De Bellis	Rustica	Insular Majuscule	Tourneure

written ♀ throughout the rest of Greece. The Etruscans used the signs φ or ♀ before the [u] sound. Only the form ♀ remained in archaic Latin (Lapis Niger, 600 BCE).

On Roman inscriptions dating from the first century, the letter Q had a gently curving but particularly long tail when it was engraved on stone, bronze (for example on the Claudian Tablet, a speech of Emperor Claudius engraved on a bronze plate, 48 CE), or other materials. This prolongation lends a supple rhythm to the otherwise solemn and somewhat austere texts of that period.

Since the Romans already had two letters to mark a [k] sound, C and K, they used the letter Q exclusively together with the letter U to indicate a [kw] sound, which abounded in Latin (demonstrated by words such as *equatus*, *quartus*, *aqua*). In Old English this sound was originally written as cw (as in *cwen*, "queen") but with the influx of French words after the Norman Conquest (1066), the spelling qu was introduced (*query*, *require*, etc.). Subsequently, the qu spelling was also

DISTURBANCE. A modern typeface based on the early forms of Greek and Etruscan letters.

The word *ki* ("who," in Old French) in the twelfth century.

Left, ROMAN CAPITAL. A section of the Claudian Tablet, 48 CE.

Followed by a colon or semicolon, the Q replaces *que*. CAROLINGIAN MINUSCULE, second half of the eighth century. To the right, the same abbreviation in TEXTURA.

The word *omnique* (and all), CAROLINGIAN MINUSCULE.

usq; the abbreviation means *usque* (until). GOTHIC TEXTURA.

	1450	1550	
Batarde	Rotunda	Humanist	—— Modern forms ——
Cursive	—— Fraktur ——	—— Chancellery ——	

DEMOCRATICA, BLUR, and
MANSON ALTERNATE, 35-point.

[1] BELLERY WIDE.

Right, from left to right:
LUBALIN, AVANT-GARDE,
COCHIN, and CASLON 224.

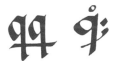

Two abbreviated forms of
the word *quoque*.

used for native English words, and *cwen* became *queen*. In modern English, the letter is still almost always followed by a u. Some exceptions are words that have been borrowed from other languages, such as *Al Qaeda*, from the Arabic, and *qi*, from the Chinese.

SHAPES & INTERPRETATIONS

In ROMAN CURSIVE script from the first and second centuries, the letter appears quite angled and does not have a bowl. In its uppercase form, the Q takes the O structure, with the addition of a line that prolongs its lower part to the right. Some see it as the image of a sprouted seed or even an ovum fertilized by a spermatozoon, which makes the letter's tail.[1]

It is also interesting to note the link established between this letter and water. Its aquatic (from the Latin *aqua*, "water") nature is quite visible in the following typographic forms:

THE LETTER IN BRIEF, ABBREVIATIONS & MEANINGS

→ In ancient Rome, the letter Q had a numeric value of 500, or 500,000 with a *titulus*.

→ In the famous inscription SPQR (*Senatus Populusque Romanus*, "the Roman senate and people"), the letter abbreviates the coupling conjunction *que* (and).

→ The doubled letter, QQ, abbreviates *quinquennalis* (every five years).

→ During the Middle Ages, the letter was the basis for the following abbreviations:

			around 1300	
que (and)	*qui* (who)	*quantum* (how much)	*quar* (for)	*qu'ele* (that she)

- → On early medical prescriptions, Q stood for *quantity* and Q.S. for *sufficient quantity*.
- → As a unit of weight, q abbreviates the word *quintal* (equal to 100 kg).
- → In mathematics, a barred Q represents the set of all rational numbers.
- → IQ stands for *intelligence quotient*.
- → In the abbreviation Q&A, Q stands for *question*.
- → Finally, Q is the only letter that does not appear in any U.S. state name.

Abbreviations for the Latin words *qui, quod,* and *quibus*.

R

FORCE RAGE RUMBLING RETURN

Eighteenth letter of the alphabet & fourteenth consonant

The Hebrew letter RESH, with a numeric value of 200.

The word for *sun*, pronounced *re* or *ra*.

The Phoenician letter RESH. The Latin words *rex* (king) and *regnum* (reign) are based on that letter's name.

The Greek letter RHO, lowercase and uppercase. When used to record numbers, it indicated 100.

ORIGIN & EVOLUTION

In the Egyptian hieroglyphic alphabet, the sign ◁▷ meant "mouth" and was used to mark the [r] sound.

But the true origin of our modern R dates back to the Proto-Sinaitic sign ℰ (*ra'chu*), representing the profile of a head. When the Phoenicians adopted this letter, they simplified it to the form ꟼ, which remained unchanged from the thirteenth to fifth century BCE. The Phoenician character bears the name RESH, which corresponds to the Hebrew word *rosh* (head) and by extension refers to the notion of "principle," derived etymologically from the Latin *principium* (beginning, origin, or cause). The same *principium* was also associated with the letter YODH (see I).

At first, the Greeks used the same design as the Semitic RESH to write their own letter RHO, before reorienting it toward the right (Ρ). By rounding out the upper part in the classical phase, they arrived at the shape of our P. In archaic Greek, RHO sometimes also resembled the letters R and D (R and D). The Etruscans, in turn, wrote R with the shape ꟼ on their oldest inscriptions. Later, they used the letter ꟼ.

The Romans, who used Ρ for P, adopted one of the Greek models (R) to write the letter R, which was always

100	400		700		800
Roman Capital	Rustica		——— Uncial ———	Roman Semi-uncial	Insular Majuscule
	De Bellis	Quadrata		Luxeuil Minuscule	Insular Minuscule

Letters eri

followed by an H in words of Greek origin, such as *rhapsody,*
rhesus, or *rheumatism.*

In spoken English the R has a tendency to be omitted
in certain words, depending on the speaker's dialect or social
class. Linguists divide between rhotic and non-rhotic pronunciation. For example, rhotic speakers would distinctly
pronounce the R in *water,* while non-rhotic speakers would
drop the R to pronounce [watah].

SHAPES & INTERPRETATIONS

As early as the first century CE, we begin to encounter the most
remarkable forms. For example, in ROMAN CURSIVE, the letter
is written ʃ. In seventh- and eighth-century MEROVINGIAN
texts, the shape of the R was similar to that of a long S (ʃ) and
was ligatured with most other letters:

ri   ro   rs   rt   ru

Starting in the eleventh century, we can observe an un-
usual form for the lowercase r. Known as a "half-r," it was at
first used only after the letter o, but subsequently came to be
used after any letter with a right-hand bowl or shoulder, such
as b, h, or p. The stem of the r consisted then of the right-
hand part of the letter preceding it.

| Primitive Gothic | Sine Pedibus | Textura | Fraktur | Fraktur | Fraktur |
| 1150 | 13th c. | 15th c. | 17th c. | 1700 | 1700 |

The monogram CHI-RHO,
symbol of the Christian faith,
formed from the first two letters
of the Greek word Χριστος
(*Christos*). In the Latin world,
it was also interpreted as *pax*
(peace).

Runic-style INSULAR MAJUSCULE.

The word *vero,* LUXEUIL
MINUSCULE, seventh and eighth
centuries.

The letters o and half-r in
GOTHIC TEXTURA.

r   o and half-r   half-r

	1100	1200		1300	
	Tourneure		Gothic	Textura	
Carolingian	— Gothic Primitive —		Textura Sine Pedibus	— Rotunda —	

Cancellarefcho Corsivo [I]

Lowercase and capital R in GOTHIC CURSIVE (fifteenth and sixteenth centuries). Note the horizontal arm (or tail) on the majuscule, normally written as a descending diagonal. Its form in GOTHIC BATARDE is nearly identical.

The abbreviation for the Latin ending -*RUM* and -*rum*.

The abbreviations for the Latin *erunt* (they will) and *eorum* (of them).

An abbreviation of the word *registered*.

Beginning in the seventeenth century, the form of the lower-case changed. In CANCELLARESCA CORSIVA[I] and the subsequent scripts known as ROUND, FLOWING, and ENGLISH, the r takes the forms ℛ ℛ ℎ, undoubtedly inspired by the shape of the "half-r."

THE LETTER IN BRIEF, ABBREVIATIONS & MEANINGS

→ In the Roman numeral system R has a value of 80 and becomes 80,000 with a *titulus*. Among the Greeks the RHO indicated the number 100.

→ The Romans nicknamed the R "the canine letter" based on its pronunciation, which evokes the sound of a growling dog.

→ In Latin inscriptions, R may stand for *Roma, Rex, Responsio,* or *Regio.* The couple RP corresponds to *Respublica* (the Republic).

→ R⁰ is the abbreviation for *recto* (the superscript letter is an o).

→ In early medical prescriptions, the letter R was used for Latin *recipe* (take).

→ Written in the margins of medieval manuscripts, R sometimes appears as the abbreviation of the Latin word *require* (look for). It helped orient the reader toward other works with complementary information.

→ In mathematics, ℝ designates the set of real numbers.

→ Rh. is the abbreviation for *rhesus*.

→ R is the symbol for röntgen, a unit of measure for X-rays or gamma rays.

ligature pr   frère (brother)

1400	1500	1800	
Gothic Batarde	Chancellery script	Flowing	Modern form
Gothic Cursive		Round	English

→ In geometry, the lowercase indicates the *radius*, for example in the formula: $P = 2\pi r$.

→ In the American film rating system (Motion Picture Association of America) R stands for *restricted*, meaning that children under seventeen must be accompanied by an adult.

→ An R enclosed within a circle (®) denotes a registered trademark.

→ In schools the three Rs, regarded as the fundamentals of education, stand for reading, writing, and arithmetic.

Celtic forms:
RUNIC MAJUSCULE and
INSULAR MAJUSCULE.

R

The French word *predeccesseurs* in GOTHIC CURSIVE, around 1530.

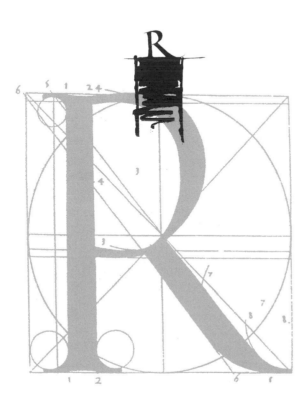

S

SINUOSITY SYMBOL
DANGER TOOTH

Nineteenth letter of the alphabet
& fifteenth consonant

The letter SHIN, with a numeric value of 300.

The Egyptian hieroglyph, shaped like a taut bow.

The Phoenician SHIN. Left, as it appeared on the Mesha Stele, ninth century BCE. Right, on King Eshmunazar's tomb, fifth century BCE.

The Hebraic SADE has a numeric value of 90, the FINAL SADE is 900.

ORIGIN & EVOLUTION

Several ancient signs were used to indicate sounds close to our S. In Egypt, three uniliteral glyphs had a similar pronunciation: ⌐ [s], ▬ [z], and ▭ [ch]. The first represents a folded cloth, the second a lock, and the third a water basin. In the Proto-Sinaitic alphabet, the sign ⌒, an ancestor of our S, may be interpreted as an image of teeth, breasts, or a bow (based on the design ⌒). That primitive sign gave birth to the second-to-last letter in the Phoenician alphabet, called SHIN and written like our W. When it was adopted into the Greek alphabet, the letter was rotated vertically and baptized SIGMA. It was written ⟨ or ⟨, or even ⟨ during the Roman period. Little by little, the first of those forms (with three strokes) gave way to the second, the Ionian form. This evolved into the classical Σ around 400 BCE.

Before we continue, let us return to the Phoenician alphabet for a moment in order to point out the existence of two other sibilant consonants, the SAMEKH ‡ [ks] and the SADE ⋔ [ts], which became the Greek alphabet's XI and SAN, respectively. The SAN, which is shaped like our M, was used in place of the SIGMA in several early Greek inscriptions. Situated between ∏ and ϙ, the letter M [s] (quickly

0		500	700		800		
Roman Capital	Rustica	Roman Semi-uncial		Artificial Uncial		Insular Majuscule	Carolingian
Pompeian graffiti		Uncial	Merovingian		Runic letter		Insular Minuscule

replaced by the SIGMA) was adopted by the Etruscans, who placed it between the letters 7 and Φ in their alphabet. Besides the SAN, which they pronounced [ch], three Etruscan signs represented the [s] sound: ⊞, derived from SAMEKH; Ⲭ based on XI [ks]; and ⟨, resulting from SIGMA. On the earliest Roman inscriptions, such as those on the Lapis Niger (see p. 17), the S was still a rather rigid character composed of three straight strokes (𝈦).

In the tenth century, the lowercase, which had been represented until then by its long form, ſ, changed to an s (short s) at the end of words. This new way of writing an s, still rare at the time, became common practice over the subsequent centuries, but the long form was still used internally in words until the sixteenth century.[1]

In written English the letter S is the most frequent one at the beginning of a word. It can take on various shades of voiced or voiceless pronunciation as the words *sun, use, usual,* and *study* demonstrate.

SHAPES & INTERPRETATIONS
Even though it was adapted to the various scripts that followed ROMAN CAPITAL (RUSTICA, UNCIAL, QUADRATA), the shape of the capital S retained its structure. This is not true of the lowercase, which changed greatly from period to period.

In ROMAN CAPITAL and in its current form, the letter is carved out of the shape of an 8. Similar to a Möbius strip or the symbol for infinity, ∞, the completeness of the numeral 8 embodies the notion of vitality, return, and eternity. This idea is illustrated concretely in painting: in order to correctly

The Greek letter SIGMA, lowercase and uppercase forms. It was used to write the number 200.

The sign for SAMPI, adopted by the Greeks to write the number 900.

[1] In CANCELLARESCA CORSIVA, or cursive chancellery script, two Ss are combined into one letter.

The unique shape of the final s in GOTHIC type.

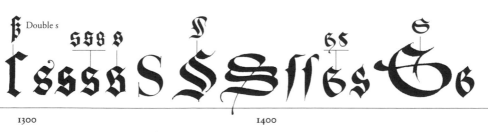

Double s

1300   1400

——— Textura ———   ——— Batarde ———

Tourneure   ——— Gothic Cursive ———

The ligature *st* in MEROVINGIAN, CAROLINGIAN, and GOTHIC forms.

[2] The *tai-chi-tu* is a Chinese symbol representing the complementarity of *yin* (black, feminine, passive) and *yang* (white, masculine, active). The central S represents a dragon or serpent, the source of primordial energy. This design shows a balance between opposing elements.

Right, two forms for the final s in *les gens des trois estats* (the people of the three estates) the final s in the word *juges* (judges), and the *st* ligature in the word *administration*, GOTHIC CURSIVE, 1523.

Different ligatures in CHANCELLERY script.

blend colors, pigments are crushed with a pestle moved in the shape of an 8. In the lowercase, the long s is distinct from the f because it lacks a cross stroke and often has a shorter stem than the f.

The letter garners its essential strength from its spine, which divides a circle perfectly into two equal parts. This characteristic can be found in the symbol known as a *tai-chi-tu*.[2] Composed exclusively of curving lines, the shape of the S espouses suppleness and grace. In fact, there is a great sensuality in this elegance, which one could qualify as "feminine." However, its shape also leads to more negative connotations when it is compared to a serpent, to lightning, or the staggering sway of a drunkard. Words such as *hiss*, *sin*, *Satan* express its menacing connotation.

	Double s	**1500**	Double s
Rotunda		Humanist Round and Cursive	
Fraktur			Modern forms

THE LETTER IN BRIEF, ABBREVIATIONS & MEANINGS

→ In antiquity, an S had a numeric value of 7 or 70. With a *titulus*, it became 7,000 or 70,000.

→ Other scholars attribute a value of 90 to it, or 90,000 when topped with a *titulus*. It would then be related to the SADE (which has a numeric value of 90), and not the Hebraic SHIN (which has a numeric value of 300).

→ For the Romans, the letter was a sign for silence.

→ On diplomas and charters, an S preceding the signatories' names is short for *signum* (sign).

→ On a weather vane, map, or compass S designates *south*.

→ In musical scores, it indicates *solo* (rest).

→ In Latin inscriptions, the letter S may abbreviate the following words: *Servus, Sanctus, Senatus, Scriptus, Secundus*. It is also the first letter of SPQR: *Senatus Populusque Romanus* (the senate and people of Rome).

→ Certain epitaphs bear the four-letter sequence S.T.T.L., which abbreviates *Sit tibi terra levis* (May the Earth be light upon you).

→ On early medical prescriptions, S.Q. abbreviates *sufficens quantitas* (sufficient quantity), and S. and SS., *semi*, to indicate half of a quantity. The letter S's connection to the notion of half dates far back. Until the eleventh century, it was used to indicate half of a number (VIII S = 8/2 = 4). Later, it was replaced by a symbol that strongly resembles our +.

→ As a unit of time, the lowercase s abbreviates the word *second*, not to be confused with the second of an angle, written ″. The sign ″ is also found in mathematics. Used after a letter, it indicates a double prime. Thus, the term *A″* stands for "A double prime," indicating the element following *A′* (called "A prime").

→ In physics, S abbreviates siemens, a unit for measuring electric conductance, equivalent to an ampere per volt.

→ In chemistry, S stands for sulfur (considered in ancient chemistry to be the condensation of fire).

→ SOS has been associated with *save our souls* in popular usage.

As a mathematical sign, the SIGMA abbreviates the word *sum*.

The long S form is used in math when writing functions.

INSULAR MINUSCULE, around 700. The shape of the s was often confused with an r.

The word *coulées* (flows), with a unique final s.

Road sign. Slippery road.

Abbreviation for *fortissimus* in GOTHIC TEXTURA.

The abbreviations for the words *sanctus* and *saint*.

A few ancient symbols for sulfur.

→ Crossed with two vertical strokes, the S represents the dollar.[3] Today the use of only one vertical stroke is common.

→ In marine terminology SS corresponds to *steamship* or USS to *United States ship*.

→ The word *Saints* can be abbreviated by SS, as in SS Peter and Paul.

→ The double S stood for *Schutzstaffel* during Nazi Germany.

T

EARTH TRACE SIGN

*Twentieth letter of the alphabet
& sixteenth consonant*

ORIGIN & EVOLUTION

In the Egyptian alphabet, there are two uniliteral glyphs that transcribe the [t] sound: the first resembles a loaf of bread ▬ and the second a pestle ◗. A third sign, resembling an animal's leash, ▭, makes more of a [tch] sound.

Our T derives from the last letter of the Proto-Sinaitic alphabet, called TAW, which marked the [t] sound with either a ✚ or ✗ sign. These same shapes were used by the Phoenicians to write their letter TAW, which also falls at the end of their alphabet. The Greeks adopted the Phoenician sign ✚ into their alphabet but omitted the upper portion. In this way, it became the Greek T, baptized TAU.[I]

Another Phoenician letter is worth noting since it makes a sound similar to [t]. This is the TETH [th, a more emphatic t sound], written either ⊗ or ⊕, depending on the period and region. These two shapes influenced the Greek THETA, which was also written ⊙ on the earliest inscriptions. Later, the central dot was stretched, leading the THETA to its classical form, Θ. The Etruscans also had three signs to transcribe the phonetic value [th]. The oldest, which resembles the Phoenician ⊗, was quickly abandoned in favor of O and ⊙.[2] It was impossible to confuse the consonant symbol O [th] with the vowel O since the Etruscans only used the latter in their alphabets and not in their actual texts.

Besides the Etruscan sign T, which marked the sound [t] and was derived from the Greek TAU, there was another letter with a phonetic value similar to [t], derived from both the Phoenician ZAYIN [z] and the Greek ZETA. It maintained its original form, 𐌆, but was pronounced [ts].

The Romans had no need to write the [th] sound in their language, so the Etruscan consonant O, derived from

The Hebraic TAW has a numeric value of 400. As a word *taw* means "sign," "mark," or "symbol" in Hebrew. The word *symbol* here is used in its etymological sense, meaning "throw together" or "join together."

The Phoenician TAW, Yehimilk inscription, thirteenth century BCE.

[I] Before the arrival of Y, Φ, X, Ψ, and Ω, TAU was the final letter of the Greek alphabet. This is why we find the expression *alpha to tau* in some medieval texts, instead of *alpha to omega*.

θΘ τT

The THETA was used for the number 9 and the TAU for 300.

ꟿꟻ𐌉Oꟽꟿ

[2] The Etruscan word *suthina* as it appears on a bronze mirror dating from the third century BCE. Based on the word *suthi* (tomb), it was a funeral offering and may be translated "for the tomb," read from right to left.

The letter TAW on the tomb of King Eshmunazar, fifth century BCE.

A few forms of the Etruscan T.

3 The Egyptian ANKH also represented a copper mirror. That metal was highly prized by Egyptians who imagined it had the power to retain light.

propter

The word *propter* in MEROVINGIAN script.

intelligismus habitant

4 The words *intelligismus* and *habitant*.

the Greek THETA, was left out of their alphabet. Instead, they only borrowed the T to indicate the [t] sound.

In written English T is the second most common letter (after E) and can represent various sounds. In American accents this unvoiced plosive can soften when positioned in the middle of words and be pronounced similar to a [d]. Other possible sounds are illustrated by words such as *tea, ration, thin.* The voiced and unvoiced sounds of th in *rather* and *cloth* were originally marked by their own letters in Old English manuscripts, called thorn and eth, which gradually disappeared from English spelling after the Norman conquest (when French spelling rules were adopted).

SHAPES & INTERPRETATIONS

In Egypt, the handled cross, shaped like the letter T and bearing the name ANKH, is the symbol of eternal life and health.3 It resembles the image of an upright man, arms outstretched, fully embracing life and breathing copiously.

The T has a very particular shape in the MEROVINGIAN scripts of the seventh century, where it is written ꞇ. There are also the following ligatures: ꝏ (te), ꝺ (ti), and ꝸ (tu). In texts from the eighth to tenth centuries, the letter frequently appears upside down when it follows the letter n,4 which was also the position that the letter adopted for the & sign (see Ampersand, in E). In addition, during that same period, the cross stroke on the lowercase t, placed at x-height, is often attached to the following letter. This creates the type of hybrid character that can make deciphering difficult, as is evident in the CAROLINGIAN ligatures ꞇ (ti), ꞇ (tr), and ꞇꞟ (tu).

400			700		800	
Roman Capital	Quadrata		Artificial Uncial		Insular Majuscule	
	Rustica	Uncial		Runic letter		

The uppercase T is composed of a horizontal and a vertical line. This design seems to create a link between past and future (the left and right), as well as Earth and sky (bottom and top). The letter's shape resembles the profile of a table, or even that of scales, the symbol of justice. It may recall a roof, evoking the idea of shelter or protection. Even though the T stands on the narrow base of its stem, it imparts a sense of great stability and expresses equilibrium.

THE LETTER IN BRIEF, ABBREVIATIONS & MEANINGS

→ In Antiquity, the T had a numeric value of 160 and became 160,000 with a *titulus*.

→ In Rome, the tribunes affixed a letter T (most likely the first letter of the word *testor*, "to attest") on Senate orders to indicate approval.

→ In inscriptions, the letter is used to abbreviate the words *Titus, Titius, Tullius, tibi* (to you), *titulus* (title or inscription), *terra, terminus* (limit), or *testimonium* (testament).

→ A truncated cross, shaped like a T, was worn on the clothes of the religious followers of Saint Anthony.

→ This letter also represents the T-shaped screw used to hold a knife's blade in its handle without requiring the use of a nail.

→ In surgery, the letter lends its name to bandages made up of two strips that form a T.

→ T is the abbreviation for the prefix *tera-*, which multiplies the subsequent unit by 10^{12}. It is also the symbol for tesla, a unit of magnetic induction.

PİGMEN†
A††ester

Today, certain typefaces present a cruciform t, reminiscent of its original design. MANSON and DEMOCRATICA, 24-point.

The T-square, a design tool.

Abbreviations for *ter, tum, tur, tus*.

The word *terra*, thirteenth century.

ligature st

1300   1400

Tourneure   Textura Sine Pedibus

Carolingian Minuscule   Gothic Textura   Rotunda

The abbreviated form of *alterius* (one of two, one, the other).

The abbreviation for the word *terram* (Earth).

→ The lowercase t abbreviates ton, a unit of weight.

→ On symphony scores, a T replaces the word *tutti*.

→ A lowercase t followed by a superscript O (t^o) stands for *temperature*.

→ In recipes a lowercase t stands for *teaspoon*, and a capital T for *tablespoon*.

→ The letter is used in the expression "suit you to a T."

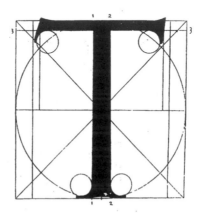

ligature ti *ultima*

1400   1500

———— Batarde ————

——— Chancellery ———

Modern forms

U & V

Twenty-first letter of the alphabet
& fifth vowel (U)
Twenty-second letter of the alphabet
& seventeenth consonant (V)

ORIGIN & EVOLUTION

The letters U, V, and W are derived from the same Proto-Sinaitic consonant WAW as the F (see F). Research on the history of our sixth letter has shown that the F was based on the Greek DIGAMMA, which itself derived from a rotated Phoenician WAW. Here, the Semitic consonant Y is adopted nearly identically by the Greeks as the twenty-third letter of their alphabet: the vowel UPSILON. That letter, with a phonetic value [y, pronounced like the German ü], was written either V or Y before it took its classical form, Y. These same three forms came to be used by the Etruscans to indicate the sound [u]. In early Latin inscriptions, such as on the Lapis Niger, the letter U is still written Y, but this shape was quickly abandoned in favor of the V, which was used both for the vowel U and the consonant V.[1]

In the first centuries CE, in certain scripts (Pompeian graffiti, ROMAN CURSIVE, RUSTICA, and UNCIAL from the fourth and fifth centuries), there was a pronounced curve in the left-hand downstroke of the letters U and V. Their form was quite close to the shape of our lowercase u.[2] The two letters maintained that shape during the centuries that followed. Starting in the ninth century, in order to avoid confusion with other letters (including the n), the u was sometime topped with a curved diacritic mark (ŭ). In the fifteenth century, this was replaced with two slightly italicized points.

From the thirteenth to fifteenth centuries, the V shape (used for both the vowel and consonant) was used primarily as the first letter of a word. As is already evident, the U and V were indistinguishable for centuries.

The first graphic differentiation of the two letters occurred in a Gothic alphabet dating from 1386 (in which the V is positioned before the U). In HUMANIST script, the V

The Hebraic WAW, with a numeric value of 6.

The Greek letter UPSILON, equivalent to 400.

The U was often replaced by an O (*volgus* for *vulgus*) and sometimes used instead of an E or I: *legundi* for *legendi* and *maxumus* for *maximus*.

[1] **SENATVS**

The letter in DE BELLIS script, first century.

On monuments, U is an abbreviation for:
Urbs (the city), *Usus* (used, or usage), *Uxor* (woman).

On some documents, the letter U bears a diacritical mark: a curved stroke in the ninth century and two italic points in the fourteenth century.

Two shapes of the letter (initial and middle position) in the word *volume*.

uero

The word *vero* (truly) in HUMANISTIC CURSIVE.

ū

U with a *titulus*, for *um*.

fructū

The word *fructum* in GOTHIC BATARDE.

úboʒ

The word *verborum*.

Ut tibi prosit meri potio (May this glass of pure wine bring you health). *Ut* is the first word of the toast that printers made when drinking.

(sometimes called a "consonant U") appeared in 1425. Several years later, in 1548, Ervé Fayard established the distinction between U (a vowel with a rounded base) and V (a pointed consonant). Pierre de la Ramée—better known as Petrus Ramus—made the same distinction in 1557. The rounded U, like the J, was not accepted as a capital letter until 1629 by the Strasbourg printer Lazare Zetzner, and it was not until 1762 that the French Academy definitively split the two letters U and V.

LETTER U:
SHAPES & INTERPRETATIONS

From a lump of clay we fashion a vase;
This empty space in the vase permits its use.
　　　　　　　　　　　　　　—Lao Tsu

The shape of the letter U, like that of its sister consonant, evokes a cup meant to receive and contain. And just as V is the first letter of *vagina*, the letter U is found twice in the word *uterus*.

Rimbaud associates the color green with this vowel. This character is therefore related to plants that acquire their coloration from chlorophyll, whose pigment has a molecular structure similar to that of hemoglobin (with magnesium instead of iron). In my opinion, the letter U also relates to the color reddish-brown: in words such as *humus, humble, rustic,* and *useful* it awakens within us a sense of the terrestrial. This notion is also connected to wood and to traditional values.

	400			700			800	
Roman Capital		Rustica		Uncial		Insular Majuscule		Carolingian
	Quadrata		Roman Uncial		Artificial Uncial		Merovingian	

When sung on the musical note C, the [u] sound acts upon our first *chakra* and creates a descending movement. Associated with the color red (as well as squares and the Earth), that point is also called the "root *chakra*."

THE LETTER IN BRIEF, ABBREVIATIONS & MEANINGS

→ In the Roman numeral system U (written V) had a value of 5, or 5,000 with a *titulus* above it.[3]

→ The letter is the chemical symbol for uranium.

→ It is the first letter of the German word *Unterseeboot* (abbreviated as *U-boot*), "submarine."

→ The letters UV abbreviate *ultraviolet*.

→ In arboriculture, U refers to the particular shape of certain fruit trees (such as apricot and peach trees), whose branches grow parallel. A simple U means two branches and a double U represents four.

→ UT is the former name of the musical note DO, the high-pitched syllable rechristened by the Italians in the seventeenth century. In Anglo-Saxon countries, this note is called C.

→ The letters U and V are often used to describe the shape of various objects: for example "a U tube," "a V-neck," or "a U-lock," which is a type of anti-theft lock for two-wheeled vehicles.

→ A circled U indicates kosher certification by the Orthodox Union.

The ligature *um* in INSULAR MAJUSCULE.

3 V = 5, as half of X, which equals 10.

The ligatures *us, ur,* and *ut* in UNCIAL.

Abbreviation for *vere dignum* (truly worthy).

Ut, first word of the hymn to Saint John the Baptist:
Ut *queant laxis,* resonare *fibris,* mira *gestorum,* famuli *tuorum,* solve *polluti,* la*bii reatum. Sancte* Ioannes (So that your servants may, with liberated voices, sing of your admirable deeds, wipe the guilt from our soiled lips, Saint John).

1000	1160		1400		
	Tourneure		Textura Sine Pedibus		Gothic Cursive
Capital		Gothic Textura		Gothic Batarde	

Triangles on point: the alchemical symbols for Earth and water.

The shape of the V, "laughing" and "positive," is used in advertisements for watches, which usually show the time 10:10.

The letter X, holding a terminal position in the word *sex*, may be broken into two triangles. The feminine one points downward and the masculine one points up. These two figures are wed in the Star of David.

LETTER V:
SHAPES & INTERPRETATIONS

The letter V has a dynamic and positive character. It seems to gush from the ground, rising up and spreading out into the air, like a spray of water. Its design, similar to a smiling mouth, expresses vitality and joy. Shaped like lifted wings, the letter initiates the words *vivacious, vivid, vehement.*

Its pronunciation is soft, caressing, and sensual. This lightness is evident in words such as *velvet, voluptuous, velour, vowel.* The sound of this consonant, which is known as a voiced labio-dental fricative, also evokes the sound of the wind, hinting at notions of speed and trembling (*velocity, vibration, vroom*).

It shares several common symbolic points with the letter U, notably in the idea of a container, evoked by its form and illustrated by words such as *vase, vessel, vial, vat, ventricle.* The word *vagina,* derived (through medieval French) from the Latin word of the same spelling, referred to a sheath, a scabbard, a case, or an envelope. The letter's shape recalls that of the Sumerian ideogram for "woman,"[4] a triangle on point with a vertical stroke representing the vulva. The protruding part of the pubic triangle is called the "mound of Venus." V is the first letter in the name of the goddess of love and beauty and the central letter in the name Eve. Somewhat paradoxically, it is also found at the beginning of the words *virile* (from the Latin *vir,* man), *vigorous,* and *valiant,* thus charged with masculine connotations. Like the letter Y, the letter V may therefore refer to the sex without specifying gender. Masculine and feminine, it has acquired an androgynous quality.

1500

——— Rotunda ——— ——— Humanist ——— ——— Modern forms ———

Fraktur ——— Chancellery ———

THE LETTER IN BRIEF, ABBREVIATIONS & MEANINGS

→ In Latin church books, where it is most often crossed, V stands for *verset* 5 (verse).

→ The pronunciation of the Latin V underwent a sound shift to [b] by about 300 CE. This is still evident in modern Spanish, where the letter V has the pronunciation [b]. The permutation of B and V is also visible in Latin manuscripts, where the word *velli* was often written for *belli* (wars), as was *Danuvius* for *Danubius* (Danube).

→ In bibliographies, V° stands for *verso* (the superscript letter is an O).

→ In World War II, the letter became a symbol of victory for the Allies, formed by the index and middle fingers.

→ In music, the V marks passages intended for the violin. You also find V for *volti* (turn) and VS for *volti subito* (turn quickly).

→ In geometry, V is the abbreviation for volume. In electricity, it stands for volt.

→ The letter is the chemical symbol for vanadium, a silvergray metal used in preparing iron and steel alloys.

→ In grammar, v or vb is an abbreviation for *verb*.

Capitals in CHANCELLERY

5 Abbreviation for *verset*.

U
V

In inscriptions, a V is often used for U:

V.R.

Urbs Romana (the city of Rome).

A.V.C.

Ad urbe condita (since the founding of the city, Rome).

The number 7 in the twelfth century, called a *zenis*.

In Ancient Rome, a V was placed next to the names of surviving soldiers, whereas a Greek Θ (THETA) indicated that they had succumbed. It was the first letter of Θανατος (death).

W

WATER DUPLICATION

*Twenty-third letter of the alphabet
& eighteenth consonant*

[1] The Egyptian letter and its more stylized form. It was pronounced [u], [o], or [w].

[2] The names of the archdeacons *Widonis* and *Warmundi*.

The letter resembling a W is, in fact, an overlapping V and U. This is the abbreviation for *vulnus* (wound), written on an Anglo-Saxon document from the twelfth century.

ORIGIN & EVOLUTION

The uniliteral Egyptian hieroglyph with a sound similar to the letter W is the image of a small quail, drawn either realistically or in a more stylized fashion.[1]

Our letter W came from the Germanic languages of the Middle Ages, in which the [w] sound abounded. It appears in texts prior to the twelfth century but only rarely. In a charter from the year 1073, for example, written in diplomatic script, the letter W is used in two proper names: *Widonis* and *Warmundi*.[2] In early German manuscripts the [w] sound was indicated by a double U, based on the fact that the u marked a [w] sound in the Latin digraph Qu [kw]. This usage of the double U was also found in Viking-occupied Normandy, France. In Anglo-Saxon England the voiced bilabial semivowel [w] was originally transcribed by a letter of their own invention, called WYN or WEN. During the Norman occupation this letter gradually vanished, replaced by the Norman double U. In the rest of France surviving [w] sounds were spelled with a U.

In the opinion of the scholar Jean Mabillon (1632–1707) it was during the twelfth century that two V's were joined to form a single letter. Since then, the W in French is found primarily in proper names or in words of foreign origin, such as English, German, or Slavic. There were several variations of

---

1400

— Gothic Batarde —

— Fraktur —

— Modern forms —

form, including: Uu, Vu, VV, and W. In the twelfth century, the letter was written Uv. In the two centuries that followed, it continued its struggle to gain admission into French dictionaries. For example, from 1798 to 1835, the few words that began with W were integrated at the end of the section dedicated to V. It was only starting in 1878 that words beginning with W were completely separated.

In an 1839 French dictionary (the Landais edition) the problems of integrating this double consonant into French are described: "We may say that this letter belongs in no way to the French alphabet; for although it may be pronounced sometimes as [v] and sometimes as [w], it hardly attains the genius of our language."

Before the advent of print the English W took the rounded shape of a double U, but printers eventually preferred a double V shape. Since the W was adapted into the French alphabet only reluctantly, the French name for the letter, double V, refers to the print shape, while the English name, double U, evokes the earlier handwritten form.

The W as the initial of the first name *Walterus*, on a charter from 1133.

A modern rendition.

SHAPES & INTERPRETATIONS

The W resembles an upside-down M. Like the latter, its shape is tied to early pictograms of water. It is, in fact, the first letter of the words *water* and *wet*.

In GOTHIC scripts, the W bears an astonishing shape; the letter's first leg is attached to the rest of the letter at the top. In FRAKTUR script, the shape of the capital W is particularly supple and wavy.[3]

THE LETTER IN BRIEF, ABBREVIATIONS & MEANINGS

→ On a compass or map, the W is used to represent the cardinal direction *west*.

→ In chemistry, it is the symbol for tungsten.

→ The letter is the symbol for watt, a unit of mechanical or electrical power.

→ A triple w stands for world wide web.

Left, *et warde de totes vertuiz* (and guard of all virtues), twelfth century.

wW	BLUR
w W	BALZAC
WW	DEMOCRATICA
*w*W	POETICA
𝖜𝖂	WITTENBERGER

3 Lowercase and uppercase FETTE FRAKTUR, 29-point.

WWW.

The three Ws are well known to net surfers, abbreviating *world wide web*.

X

STRUCTURE CROSSING DANGER

Twenty-fourth letter of the alphabet & nineteenth consonant

The Hebraic letter SAMEKH, with a numeric value of 60.

[I] The Phoenician form, on the tomb of King Ahiram.

A rare design of the Greek XI, from the first century CE.

The lowercase and uppercase XI.

ORIGIN & EVOLUTION

The origin of the letter X dates back to the Phoenician SAMEKH, which was written ⋣. Some see this as the image of a fishbone or of a tree with branches. The Hebrew word *s'mikhah*, which means "a prop" or "to support," supports the two preceding interpretations: the first would make the sign correspond to our spinal column; the second, to canes or stays. Additionally, the Latin word *adjutorium* (aid or help) was linked to the letter (see the medieval table, p. 28). In ancient Greek, the sign's layout was identical to the Phoenician SAMEKH.[I]

Various forms of the Greek alphabet coexisted at that time. One alphabet was called "blue," another "red." In the first, the sign ⲧ represented the [ks] sound and X was pronounced [kh]. In the second alphabet, the letter Ƴ was pronounced [kh], whereas X represented the [ks] sound.

In passing from Phoenician into Greek, the letter maintained the fifteenth spot in the alphabet. Losing its vertical axis, it became XI, written Ξ in its classical version. It has a phonetic value of [ks].

Its numerical value is the same as that of the SAMEKH. When counting in hundreds, it corresponds to the CHI (χ, X) with a value of 600.

0	400	700		800	1100	1300
Roman Capital	Roman Semi-uncial		Artificial Uncial	Carolingian		Gothic Textura
	Rustica	Uncial		Merovingian	Tourneure	

The Etruscans used the Ionian form, ⊞, but added two vertical strokes, resulting in the shape ⊞. In this form, which did not survive the transition into the Latin alphabet, it marked the [s] sound. They also used the ✗ sign to represent [ks].

For a long time the X was the final letter in the Latin alphabet. Toward the beginning of the first century BCE (around the time of Cicero), the letters Y and Z were reintroduced, and the X was relegated to its third-to-last position.

The letter X never appears on its own in Latin texts during the first centuries CE; there, it is always accompanied by an S. For example, you find the word *auxsilium* for *auxilium*. The Romans, in fact, often interchanged the S and X, so you find *nixus* in place of *nisus* (childbirth, labor pain), *mistus* for *mixtus* (mixed), and *Ulyxes* for *Ulysses*.

In English spelling the letter notes the consonant grouping [gz] and [ks] in words such as *existence* or *axe* and a palatoalveolar fricative in words such as *anxious* and *obnoxious*. It is the least used letter appearing at the beginning of English words; most words starting with an X are derived from ancient Greek.

SHAPES & INTERPRETATIONS

The letter represents a cross, so its symbolism is one of both life and death. Whereas for the Egyptians, the sign meant "to break," it signified "to protect" in Mesopotamia.

The X is also present in the Christian monogram composed of the letters CHI and RHO, which comes from the word Χριστος, *Christos*. Some also interpret this symbol with its interlacing letters as a P and X, from the Latin word *pax* (peace).

Fifth-century RUSTICA. The second shape is quite rare.

GOTHIC CURSIVE, 1522.

The curved shape of ROTUNDA, fifteenth century.

The monogram for Christ. A symbol containing the Greek letters CHI and RHO.

1400

1500

Gothic Cursive

Humanist

Modern form

Batarde

Gothic initial

Chancellery

GOTHIC CURSIVE, circa 1530.

Based on the acrophonic principle, according to which a word is replaced by its initial, the letter X (CHI) was used in Greece for 1,000 (χιλιοι, *khilion*, thousand). The same symbol was used by the Romans and Etruscans for the number 10.

Above, abbreviations for the words *dixit* (he says), *septuaginta* (seventy), and *decem* (ten).

The layout of the cross, with its two angled crossbeams, gives the X a solid, stable structure. It resembles various objects, such as a simple stool, a chair, or a bench. The letter's two strokes cross slightly above its geometric center, at the height of a point called the optical center.[2]

Today, an X stands for a prohibition or danger. In mathematics, x is the sign for multiplication.

The shape of the letter's cross may be interpreted in two different ways. On one hand, we see radiance (moving toward the exterior). On the other hand, the letter seems to attract our attention to a central point (the location of a compass point) that is precisely situated at the crossing of those two strokes. Historically, the letter almost always appears in the form of a crossed X, both in the lowercase and uppercase.

THE LETTER IN BRIEF, ABBREVIATIONS & MEANINGS

→ As a numeric letter, X is worth 10. Lying on its side or with a *titulus* above it, it becomes 10,000. This last value was also written X. MILL., abbreviating *decem millia*. The abbreviation X.P. was also used for *decem pondo*, the weight of ten pounds.

→ The letter X designates a stranger (Mr. X, complaint against X). It is also used as a signature by people who are unable to write. In the Middle Ages the X represented a cross and indicated a Christian signatory. Jewish people used a circle. The letter is also used as an abbreviation for Christ (X-mas).

→ The Greek word *xenon* means "foreign thing." It is used as a prefix in the words *xenocryst* (a crystal that is not native to the rock containing it), *xenograft* (a graft of tissue from someone other than the receiver), *xenophile*, and *xenophobe*.

→ X-rays owe their name to the fact that, initially, they could not be identified; the letter X was used to indicate a still unknown value. X-rays are a form of electromagnetic radiation with a weak wavelength. They have the property of passing through matter with relative ease.

→ Due to its structure, which connects two opposing forces, the letter has a negative connotation. This is evident in expressions such as "to cross swords" as well as in superstitions like not crossing flatware in a table setting. There are also several graphical representations.[3]

→ In France, a film rated X is of a pornographic nature (the letter is found in the word *sexe*, "sex"). Here, the letter is a mark of the forbidden, and may be considered as a sort of barrier. In the U.S. X-rating has been replaced by the Motion Picture Association of America's NC-17.

→ The letter is used increasingly today to attract public attention. It is found for example in *Xbox* or the series *X-Files*.

→ Its form serves to block, cancel, or annul, hence the expressions "to cross something out" and "to X out."

→ In biology the letter designates a chromosome. Doubly present in women (XX), it is accompanied by a Y in men (XY).

→ In mathematics the symbol x denotes the multiplication of two numbers.

→ In informal written communication a lowercase x represents a kiss.

A road sign indicating a crossing and a risk of danger.

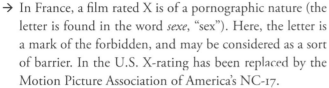

Modern form.

Y

FEMININITY PYTHAGORAS
RECEPTIVE

*Twenty-fifth letter of the alphabet
& sixth vowel*

The Hebraic WAW, with a
numeric value of 6.

The two main forms for the
Phoenician WAW.

The letter UPSILON had a
numeric value of 400.

A pointed form in CAROLINGIAN
MINUSCULE.

IRISH SEMI-UNCIAL, eighth century.

ORIGIN & EVOLUTION

The Egyptian sign with a single-consonant phonetic value transcribing [y] represents two sprouted reeds ‖. In its more stylized form, it was written ＼＼.

This same [y] sound corresponds to the Proto-Sinaitic letter YODH, shaped like a forearm (see I). Our letter Y comes from both the Phoenician consonant WAW Y (see F) and the Greek UPSILON (vowel). Before being fixed in its classical form, Y, the UPSILON was written V, Y, or Y during the eighth and seventh centuries BCE, both in Crete and in Athens. The Etruscans inherited these signs and used them to write the sounds [u] or [o], though this second sound was not included in their texts (see O). On the Lapis Niger, found in the Roman Forum (600 BCE), the letter Y appears in place of the letter U (after the letter Q).

After disappearing for several centuries, both the Y and Z were reintroduced into the Latin alphabet around the middle of the first century CE in order to transcribe words of Greek origin. This fact is commemorated in the French and Spanish names for the Y (*i grec* and *i griega*).

Starting in the sixth century, the Y was written with an accent mark to distinguish it from the digraph ij (the letters

400	500	700	1100	1400
Rustica		Merovingian	Gothic Textura	
	Uncial		Carolingian	Batarde

not dotted at that time), a pair that was often present in Germanic and Dutch texts.

The Y and U have often been transposed in Latin. You find the word *Sylla*, for example, instead of *Sulla* (for Lucius Cornelius Sulla, a member of the prominent *gens Cornelia* (Cornelia family) or *satyra* in the place of *satura* (satire, a type of poetry).

In Middle English the Y often replaced the vowel I in spelling. Under French influence after the Norman conquest Y also began to be used in place of the Old English letter YOGH, which represented the semi-vowel Y in words such as *yes, yard, yawn*. In modern English Y can still represent both a vowel (*very, glyph, typography*) and a palatal semi-vowel (*yesterday, player*).

SHAPES & INTERPRETATIONS

In Antiquity, the Y was often called Pythagoras's letter or the tree of Samos (because the philosopher was born on the island of Samos). The comparison with a tree finds resonance in the letter's "branches," the letter's upper strokes.

Its shape has inspired countless authors, who confer symbolic value on it:

> *Men walk together on a common path until it splits in two, some bravely take the right-hand path, which is difficult and narrow; it is hard, rough, and precipitous, but will lead to wisdom and virtue. Others take the left-hand trail, which is wider, easier, and welcoming; sown with flowers, it leads to the abyss of vices.*[1]

MEROVINGIAN script from the seventh century.

Cursive forms.

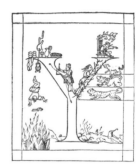

[1] The letter's symbolism. The character's branches form a V, interpreted here as *volupté* ("sensual pleasure," on the left) and *vertu* ("virtue," on the right), in *Champ Fleury* by Geoffroy Tory.

1500

Rotunda

Modern form

Fraktur

Chancellery

symeon

The word *symeon*, in
CAROLINGIAN MINUSCULE.

Y Ẏ Y

[2] Anthropomorphic aspects of the letter. The third sign is the symbol of humanity.

Right, *Royaume de France* in
GOTHIC CURSIVE.

Y

DEMOCRATICA, 30-point.
More than 3000 years have passed since the dawn of the alphabet, and the letter Y is still reminiscent of its original form, the Semitic WAW.

The Y sign is shaped like a V in its upper half, recalling the form of female genitalia. Below, it extends into a stem that could be considered symbolic of the opposite sex. With its balanced and dynamic design, the letter seems to embody the stylized image of a loving relationship. It also symbolizes the androgyny of Primordial Man, known as "Adam Kadmon."

You can also discern a sense of joy, happiness, and health in the letter Y, based on the human silhouette that it seems to reproduce.[2] These notions are found in the interjections *yay!* and *hurray.*

Royaume de France

THE LETTER IN BRIEF, ABBREVIATIONS & MEANINGS

→ For the Romans and during the Middle Ages, the Y had a numeric value of 150. With a *titulus*, it became 150,000.

→ In chemistry, it is the symbol of yttrium, a metal common to rare-earth minerals.

→ Y is a chromosome that is present in men and male mammals (XY). It is not present in females (XX).

→ The letter is an unknown quantity in algebra, coupled with X.

→ A type of moth that resembles a caterpillar and eats mint leaves is known by this letter because of a bright mark shaped like the letter Y on its wings.

→ The Y-axis is the vertical axis in plane geometry.

→ The letter is used as an abbreviation for year and yard.

→ The Y in CMYK color space stands for yellow.

Z

LIGHTNING SLITHER FIREARM

Twenty-sixth & final letter of the alphabet, twentieth consonant

ORIGIN & EVOLUTION

In Egypt, the uniliteral hieroglyph with a phonetic value similar to [z] looks like a lock or bolt ——•——. According to the linguist Émile Benveniste, another Egyptian sign can be associated with the letter Z because of its form and evolution. Pronounced [st], it originally represented an arrow piercing an animal skin, before it was simplified to the image of an arrow. As it grew more stylized, it appeared in the form, which was then rotated vertically to produce an I. In the Proto-Sinaitic alphabet, it was reduced to two parallel strokes.

The predecessor of our letter Z was written by the Phoenicians. It was the seventh letter of their alphabet and bore the name ZAYIN. Its numeric value was 7 among the Hebrews, the same value ZETA held for the Greeks.

Its sinuous structure appears in ancient Aramaic writings (eighth century BCE) and then in Phoenician script (sixth century BCE). In the earliest Greek inscriptions, the ZETA still maintained its late Phoenician form, **I**. By italicizing the stem, the Greeks arrived at its classical form, Z.

The Etruscans used the Phoenician ZAYIN (**I**) to write down the phonetic sound [ts], which we find in the words *tsar* and *tsunami*.

The Latin world adopted the Greek ZETA at the beginning of the first century BCE, often replacing it with s, ss, sd, or ds in words of Greek origin. The Greek words Ζαχυνφος, πατρζω, and Εζρας thus were written *Sachynthus* (Zakynthos, an island in the Ionian Sea), *patrisso* (to act as father), and *Esdras* (the name of a Jewish priest in the fifth century BCE).

In written English Z is the most rarely used letter. It transcribes the voiced alveolar sibilant [z] (*zodiac, prize*)

Egyptian hieroglyph.

The Phoenician form, from the Mesha Stele, ninth century BCE.

The Hebraic ZAYIN, with a numeric value of 7.

The Greek letter ZETA.

but can also represent a fricative in words such as *seizure*. In Spanish, Italian, and German, the Z is pronounced as a double letter: [ds], [dz], or [ts].

SHAPES & INTERPRETATIONS

Resembling a bolt of lightning, the Z establishes a link between Earth and sky. The sharp nature of its angles establish it as a formidable character, full of force and vigor. Its rarity in English spelling contributes to the letter's exoticness.

In early GOTHIC scripts, the ampersand was sometimes written as a numeral 2, quite similar to the Z. In FRAKTUR script, one of the versions of Z resembles the numeral 3. In the character **ꝗ**, an abbreviation for *que*, the second part could be mistaken for our final letter. It is in fact a semicolon (see Q).

A GOTHIC ampersand.

The word *scandalizatur*, LUXEUIL MINUSCULE, seventh and eighth centuries.

300	400		800		1400	
Quadrata		Carolingian			Gothic	
	Rustica		Insular Majuscule			Rotunda

THE LETTER IN BRIEF, ABBREVIATIONS & MEANINGS

→ In Greek manuscripts, Z abbreviates the word Ζητει (search), which marked suspect passages.

→ In Antiquity, the letter had a numeric value of 2,000. With a *titulus*, it became 2,000,000.

→ In fortune telling, a Z was a sign of bad luck since it represented the jaggedness of lightning. The letter's shape was also associated with the mask of death (*rictus*). In this context it is interesting to note that our last consonant is the first letter of the Etruscan word *ziva*, which meant "dead" or "deceased."

→ Z represents the third coordinate in euclidean space (after x and y).

→ With a double stem ℤ is the mathematical symbol for the set of all integers.

→ Because of its sound, the repeated letter (ZZZ) evokes the hum of a machine, the flight of an insect, or snoring (ZZZ ZZZ).

→ In the word *bizarre* the letter evokes strangeness. Its eccentric nature is also visible in words such as *crazy, zany, geezer*.

→ The term *zigzag* fully expresses the jaggedness of this letter.

→ On road signs, its shape warns of skidding or sliding.[1]

→ In "Z for Zorro," the trademark of the hero Zorro, created by Johnston McCulley, the letter is a mark of speed and precision (like lightning).

→ In the word *zipper*, a type of fastening device, the Z also represents speed.

Three abbreviations of the Latin word *est*.

FRAKTUR forms from 1150 and 1620.

Z is the first letter of *zero*, derived from the Arabic *sifr* (empty). The Italians transcribed this word as *zefiro*, which was contracted to *zero*.

1500

————— Fraktur —————

————— Chancellery —————

Modern form

The image of a lightning bolt: high voltage, DANGER!

A modern rendition, drawn with a brush.

→ The Z sound also evokes rapidity in the verb *to zap* and the interjection *zoom*.

→ A passage in *King Lear* indicates that the letter was regarded as superfluous in Shakespearean English: "Thou whoreson zed! Thou unnecessary letter!" (II.ii)

→ As the final letter of the alphabet, the Z expresses the end of something (from A to Z). Yet elsewhere, the letter is a symbol of life. This is evident in the prefix *zoo* (derived from the Greek word for "animal" or "living being") as well as in the first name Zoe, from the Greek word for "life."

Coupar difféantar de la Plume.

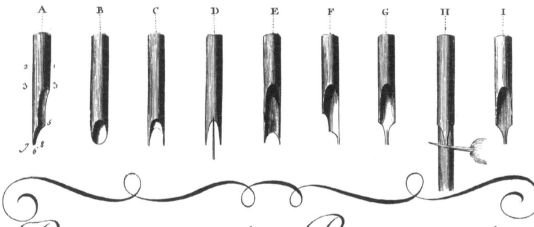

Proportions d'une Plume taillée

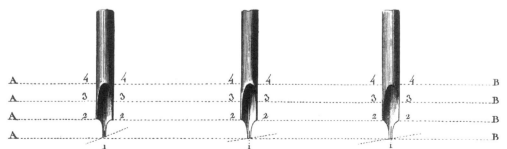

Top row: Various cuts of a quill.
Bottom row: Proportions of a cut quill.

ABBREVIATION

ALDINE

ALPHABET

ANTIPHONARY

APEX

AWL

BATARDE

BENEVENTAINE

BLACK

BODY SIZE

BOUSTROPHEDON

CALAMUS

CANIVET

CHANCELLERY

CODEX

COLOPHON

COMMA

CORPUS

CURSIVE

DEM OTIC

DOWNSTROKE

DUCTUS

EM QUAD

ENGLISH SCRIPT

EPIGRAPHY

EX LIBRIS

EXPLICIT

FILLET

FLOURISH

FOOT

FRAKTUR

GALL

GALL NUT

GARAMOND

GLOSS

GOLDEN NUMBER

GOTHIC

GRAMMAGE

GUM

GUTENBERG

HIERATIC

HIEROGLYPHS

HUMANA

HUMANISTIC

IBIDEM

IDEOGRAM

ILLUMINATION

INCIPIT

INCUNABULUM

INK

ITALICS

KNOTWORK

LAID PAPER

LINEAL

LOWERCASE

MADDER

MAJUSCULE

MANUSCRIPT

MINIATURE

MINUSCULE

ORNAMENTAL CAPITAL

PAGE RECTANGLE

PALEOGRAPHY

PALIMPSEST

PAPYRUS

PARAPH

PETROGLYPH

PICTOGRAM

PIED-DE-MOUCHE

PIGMENT

QUADRATA

QUIRE

QUOTATION MARKS

RECTO

ROMAN

ROTULUS

ROTUNDA

ROUNDHAND

RUBRIC

RUBRICATOR

RUPESTRAL

RUSTICA

SANDARAC

SCHWABACHER

SCRIBE

SCRIPT

SEMI-UNCIAL

SERIF

SET WIDTH

STYLUS

SUBSTANCE

TAIL

TEXTURA

THICK

THIN

TITIVILLUS

TITULUS

TOURNEURE

TYPE CHARACTER

TYPECASE

TYPOGRAPHY

TYPOGRAPHIC RULER

UNCIAL

UPPERCASE

UPSTROKE

VELLUM

VERSO

VIGNETTE

VISIGOTHIC

VITRIOL

VOLUMEN

VOLUTE

VOWELS

WATERMARK

WIRE-MARKS

XYLOGRAPHY

YCIAR

ZOOMORPH

GLOSSARY

ABBREVIATION: The graphic reduction of one or more words. An abbreviation may take one of several forms:
1. suspension: īb for *ibidem*
2. superscript letters: q̊d for *quod*
3. contraction: tp̄m for *temporum*
4. special signs: Ꝑ is equivalent to *per*
These are signs that copyists use to indicate the omission of one or more letters in a word.

ALDINE: The former term for italics, based on the name of Aldus Manutius, a famous Italian printer from the sixteenth century.

ALPHABET: Formed from the names of the first two letters of the Phoenician alphabet, ALEPH and BETH (which became ALPHA and BETA in Greek), it is the conventionally ordered set of letters used to write down the sounds of a given language.

ANTIPHONARY: From the Greek *antiphonos* (responding to). Another name for a Gradual, a book containing hymns, psalms, and liturgical songs for religious mass.

APEX: The upstroke ending at the top of a letter's stem. In the plural, *apices*.

AWL: A pointed metal tool used for perforating parchment in order to trace the page layout. In this way, the lines are drawn on both sides of the page in one procedure.

BATARDE:
1. A cursive GOTHIC script from the fifteenth century. Its lively and rigid design was highly appreciated in Flanders and at the court of the dukes of Burgundy.

2. A rather sober script from the seventeenth century, inclining gently to the right.

BENEVENTAINE: An Italian script that first appeared in the eighth century at the Benedictine abbey of Montecassino.

The abbreviations for *um* and the word *liber* (book).

The letters ALEPH and BETH.

An antiphonary from the fifteenth century.

abcdefghijklmn
abcdefghijklm

Granjon and *Garamond*, 16-
point.

characteribus

BLACK: From the Indo-European root *bhleg* (to burn, to gleam). The characteristic of a body whose surface absorbs all the colors of the visible spectrum.

BODY SIZE: A character's body corresponds to its printed part, in relief. A letter's x-height generally designates the height of the shorter minuscules, in other words the letters with no ascender or descender. Each character type has its own body size (small, medium, large), determined by the relationship between the x-height and the ascender or descender.

BOUSTROPHEDON: From the Greek *bous* (ox) and *strephein* (to turn). A system of writing whereby successive lines are written alternately from left to right and right to left.

CALAMUS: A reed cut and shaped for writing.

CANIVET or GANIVET: An early surgical tool shaped like a small pocket-knife, or *canif.* A small metal blade attached to a handle used to cut quills.

CHANCELLERY: CHANCELLERY script. A cursive-style script that arose in the fifteenth century. A product of the pontifical chancelleries in Rome, this script served as the model for italic characters. Also called CHANCERY.

CODEX: A book composed of a set of pages that are folded and assembled into several sets, then bound together. The plural form is *codices.*

COLOPHON:

1. An editor's or printer's trademark, included on the title page or on the cover of a book.

2. The information placed on the back of the title page or on the last page of a book, including the date and place the book was published as well as the name and address of the publisher.

COMMA: From the Greek *komma* (segment, clause).

CORPUS: The vertical height of typographic characters. During the period of lead characters, the corpus included the typeface letter plus the letter's header and footer space. The corpus could also be determined by measuring the vertical space separating the letter base of two single-spaced lines. The character's size is measured in *picas* in the United States and Great Britain, and in *Didots* in Europe.

CURSIVE: From the Latin *currere* (to run). Used to describe a quickly written script containing numerous ligatures.

DEMOTIC: From the Greek *demotikos*, from *demos* (the people). A cursive script in ancient Egypt, used from the seventh century BCE to the fifth century CE.

DOWNSTROKE: The vertical or angled stroke on certain lowercase letters that falls below the writing line. It is also called a descender (from the Latin *descendere*, "to descend").

DUCTUS: From the Latin *ducere* (to lead). The ductus determines the order and direction of the strokes used to form the different parts of a letter.

EM QUAD or EM QUADRAT: A lead or cast-iron cube equal in width to the body of type chosen. It was most often used to mark an indent after a break.

ENGLISH SCRIPT: A fine, elegant script from the nineteenth century that leans slightly toward the right. The finer upstrokes and thicker downstrokes are created by changes in quill pressure.

EPIGRAPHY: From the Greek *epigraphē* (inscription). The science that studies inscriptions engraved on lasting media such as wood, stone, metal, pottery, etc.

EX LIBRIS: A small print label, often including a name, affixed to a book to indicate the owner. It may also designate the decorative motif placed by book collectors inside the front cover of their books.

EXPLICIT: From the Latin *explicare* (to unfold), originally used to refer to the last lines of a text written on a scroll (*rotulus*). The term was then extended to refer to all manuscript texts. The phrases most often found at the

Cincq cens vingt et trois (five hundred and twenty-three).

a b c d e f g h i k l m n u m o p q

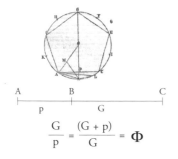

A   B   C

p   G

$$\frac{G}{p} = \frac{(G + p)}{G} = \Phi$$

end of texts were *explicit liber* and *explicitus est liber*, which translate respectively as "the book ends" or "the book ends here."

FILLET: A straight line used to extend an ornamental capital letter. A vertical or horizontal line. Varying in thickness, the fillet is meant to decorate the page and reinforce its layout.

FLOURISH: From the Latin *florere* (to bloom). This refers to the supplemental strokes attached to certain letters.

FOOT: The name given to the base of a letter's stem. Also the lower margin of a page.

FRAKTUR: From the Latin *fractura*, from *frangere* (to break). A type of GOTHIC script. The earliest known example appears in Leonhard Wagner's work *Proba centum scripturarum,* in 1507.

GALL: The gall nut, produced when an insect (*Cynips gallae tinctoriae*, gall wasp) bores into the sprouts on young oaks, is a brownish-black sphere, with a rough and bumpy texture. Its tannin can be extracted and mixed with iron or copper sulfate, gum arabic, and water in order to create ferric inks.

GALL NUT: also called an Alep nut (see map on p. 156). A growth appearing on the leaves of certain oaks.

GARAMOND, Claude: A French engraver and founder (1480–1561). He was commissioned by Francis I to create a type of Greek characters that became known as "royal." In 1534, he created an elegant typeface based on ROMAN CAPITALS, called GARAMOND.

GLOSS: From the Latin *glosa,* derived from the Greek *glossa* (language). Notes and commentaries included in a text in order to make it more intelligible.

GOLDEN NUMBER: Abbreviated by the Greek letter PHI (Φ), it has a value of 1.618. The number is used in dividing segment so that the ratio between the larger and smaller parts is equivalent to the ratio between the whole segment and the larger part. This relationship, called a "golden section," is found in nature and growth phenomena. It is well known to painters, architects, and graphic artists interested in creating a certain harmony. "Using the golden section gives the impression of rest, security, constancy in an indefinitely continuous rhythm."—R. Bouveresse

GOTHIC: The set of scripts characterized by broken letter strokes, assumed to be the result of asymmetrical quills (beveled on the left). The characters are narrower than those of the CAROLINGIAN MINUSCULE that preceded them, and abbreviations are numerous. The first texts rewritten into GOTHIC script date from around 1070 in northern France.

GRAMMAGE: Measurement corresponding to the weight of one sheet of paper cut in a square meter.

GUM: The clear, thick, viscous resin that seeps out of certain trees. It is used as a binding agent in pigments (for gouache, watercolors, etc.). Among the most common gums are gum adragant, gum arabic, and gum sandarac.

GUTENBERG, Johannes: His name means "good mountain" in German and comes from his mother's side of the family. A goldsmith by trade, he established the process for printing with movable type in Strasbourg around 1440. His real name was Johannes Gensfleisch, and in 1455, he published a magnificent Bible, also known as the 42-Line Bible. The typeface he used perfectly imitates GOTHIC TEXTURA manuscript. The text was composed with recesses, which illuminators filled with ornamental letters.

HIERATIC: From the Greek *hieratikos* (related to the sacred). Designates a white and extremely fine papyrus of superior quality, reserved for writing sacred texts. Also the cursive script of ancient Egypt.

HIEROGLYPHS: From the Greek *hieros* (sacred) and *gluphein* (to engrave). A type of writing used in ancient Egypt, appearing around 3000 BCE. Hieroglyphs can be divided into three groups:

GOTHIC TEXTURA, fifteenth century.

Crystals of gum arabic.

Portrait of Gutenberg, by André Thevet, 1584.

Sed neq3 adepti sūt i
rūt: quia ueritas idel
sensibus nō potest co
cōsilia & dispositions

De opere tercie diei

INCUNABULUM: the
Nuremberg Chronicle.

1. logographs: representing words
2. phonetic glyphs: representing sounds and functioning as a sort of picture puzzle
3. determinatives: used for narrowing the meaning of a word.

HUMANA: Character types inspired by the HUMANISTIC scripts.

HUMANISTIC: *Littera humanistica*, also called HUMANIST. A type of script developed by the Italian humanists of the Renaissance. Its layout is based on the letter structure of CAROLINGIAN MINUSCULE. Its invention is attributed to the Venetian calligrapher Poggio Bracciolini (around 1402). The humanistic shapes were adopted by the printers Conrad Sweynheym and Arnold Pannartz who, in 1465, developed the first Roman characters in the Subiaco Monastery, not far from Rome.

IBIDEM: A Latin term meaning "in the same place." Abridged as *ibid.*, it prevents the need to repeat the name of a cited work.

IDEOGRAM: From the Greek *idea* (idea) and *gramma* (written letter). A sign or character representing an idea or concept. Egyptian hieroglyphic writing is composed of ideograms.

ILLUMINATION: From the Latin *illuminare* (to light up). The richly colored letters or decorations used in manuscripts and printed texts. Space in a manuscript was reserved (in the place for an ornamental capital, for example), so that the illuminator could later "bring to light" the text.

INCIPIT: The term referring to the first words of a text.

INCUNABULUM: From the Latin *incunabula* (cradle). A text printed prior to 1501.

INK: From the Low Latin, *encautum* or *encaustum*, borrowed from the Greek *egkauston*. The Latin term primarily meant "an encaustic for painting," then "the red ink used by emperors." A pigmented liquid or paste used for writing, printing, and illustration. The same root forms the words *encre* (in French) and *inchiostro* (in Italian).

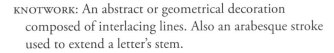

ITALICS: From the Latin *italicus*. A term used to describe writing or script that leans to the right. Originally called *Aldine*, which is derived from the name of its Venetian inventor, Aldus Manutius.

KNOTWORK: An abstract or geometrical decoration composed of interlacing lines. Also an arabesque stroke used to extend a letter's stem.

LAID PAPER: A type of paper produced with wire-marks or ribbing.

LINEAL: A character devoid of serifs, with no variation in stroke width. Lineal type is also called *sans serif* in England, *grotesk* in Germany, and *antique* or *bâton* in France.

LOWERCASE: Another name for minuscule letters, named after the lower part of a printing case, the compartmented rack in which printing letters were arranged. More frequently used than majuscules, the minuscules were placed in the lower cases, helping them to stay in place and preventing extra work for the printer.

MADDER: A plant of the *Rubiaceae* family. Alizarin is a bright red pigment extracted from its roots.

MAJUSCULE: From the Latin *majusculus* (rather large). Uppercase or capital letters.

MANUSCRIPT: From the Latin *manus* (hand). A work or document written entirely by hand.

MINIATURE: From the Latin *miniatura* and *minium*, signifying a reddish-colored lead oxide. A richly executed letter or image used to decorate manuscripts or the surfaces of various objects (boxes, snuff boxes, or jewelry).

MINUSCULE: From the Latin *minusculus* (rather small). Lowercase letters.

ORNAMENTAL CAPITAL: The larger, richly decorated or soberly designed letters used at the beginning of chapters or paragraphs.

PAGE RECTANGLE: The rectangle that defines a text's writing or printing space. It was traditionally placed slightly higher than the middle of the page and horizontally off-center to the left.

PALEOGRAPHY: From the Greek *palaios* (ancient). The science concerned with deciphering and interpreting ancient writing.

PALIMPSEST: From the Greek *palimpsestos* (scraped again). A manuscript written on parchment that is reused, the original text having been erased.

PAPYRUS: From the Greek *papuros* (Egyptian reed). A plant that grows on the banks of the Nile and other central African rivers. Papyrus stems are used to produce writing surfaces, called by the same name. First cut into small bands, they are then woven and pressed in order to produce as flat a surface as possible.

PARAPH: A decorative flourish used to extend the outline of certain letters or to terminate a signature. The abbreviated form of a signature is generally composed of the first and last initials.

PETROGLYPH: From the Greek *petra* (rock) and *gluptos* (carving). An inscription carved into rock. Also a wall or rock engraving.

PICTOGRAM: A figurative element with a stylized form that resembles what it signifies.

PIED-DE-MOUCHE: On manuscripts, this term designates the decorative designs added by copyists to the body of certain majuscules, most often in red or blue. The sign is also used to indicate a reference or the separation of paragraphs, written ¶.

PIGMENT: From the Latin *pigmentum*, from *pingere* (to paint). A powder extracted from animal, vegetable, or mineral sources used to create watercolors, inks, gouaches, etc. Pigments are held together with "binders" such as gum arabic, egg whites or yolks, synthetic resins, or glues.

MANSON ALTERNATE, 30-point.

QUADRATA: A fourth-century script based on ROMAN CAPITAL engravings. Particularly difficult to execute, it was reserved for luxury editions. The A appears with no crossbar, and the stem of the R is slightly inclined.

QUIRE: A quantity of paper, corresponding to twenty-five sheets or one-twentieth of a ream.

QUOTATION MARKS: The double marks used to isolate a word or group of words. There are two types, each with its "opening" and "closing" forms: The Americans and English use " and " and the French use « and ».

RECTO: The first side of a page, the second being the verso.

ROMAN: A character with vertical stems. If the stems are inclined, the characters are called italics. The first ROMAN characters date from 1465, created in the Subiaco Monastery, not far from Rome.

ROTULUS: A parchment or papyrus scroll. Another name for a *volumen*.

ROTUNDA: ITALIAN GOTHIC from the fourteenth century. Its shape is rounder than in other GOTHIC scripts. It was quite fashionable in Spain and southern France, and was used to print Saint Thomas Aquinas's *Summa Theologica*.

ROUNDHAND: A type of script used in the eighteenth and nineteenth centuries.

RUBRIC: From the Latin *rubrica* (red clay) and *rubeus* (red). The letters or parts of texts (usually titles) written in red ink.

RUBRICATOR: The copyist in charge of writing the letters and those parts of the text that appear in red.

RUPESTRAL: From the Latin *rupes* (rock). Referring to anything drawn, painted, or carved on a rock wall.

RUSTICA: A script that imitates the shapes of engraved ROMAN capitals. Written with a calamus or quill whose tip forms a 70-degree angle with the horizontal, it is recognizable by its very fine stems and much thicker bars.

There are two types of RUSTICA: the first-century type, which was rather thick and simple in shape, and the fifth-century type, which was lighter and more refined. Like UNCIAL, it was used as a majuscule for CAROLINGIAN script.

SANDARAC: A resin extracted from the tree of the same name in Africa and Canada. The resin is used to produce varnishes in lithography and photo-engraving.

SCHWABACHER: A type of GOTHIC script, larger than TEXTURA. It was used in Germany starting in 1474.

SCRIBE: In the fourteenth century, the term meant "a doctor of law" among the ancient Jews. In the following century, it acquired the meaning of "copyist," based on the Latin words *scriba* (writer) and *scribere* (to write). In ancient Egypt, a scribe was a public servant in charge of copying judicial, administrative, or religious documents.

SCRIPT: The image of language. The conventional graphic system that a culture adopts to represent language in a lasting fashion. Also the graphic style adopted for this representation (a script can be italic, cursive, elegant).

SEMI-UNCIAL: A type of script from the sixth century, derived from EPITOME. It was the basis for CAROLINGIAN MINUSCULE. Not to be confused with IRISH SEMI-UNCIAL, used for transcribing the Book of Kells, Lindisfarne Gospels and the Book of Durrow.

SERIF: The base of a letter's stem. In 1921, Francis Thibaudeau proposed a system for classifying characters based on their serifs. He differentiated four main letter families:
1. BATONS: no serifs
2. DIDOTS: simple lines as serifs
3. ELZEVIRS: triangular serifs
4. EGYPTIANS: squared serifs

SET WIDTH: The lateral width of a letter and its surrounding space. An M is wider than an I.

The word *baptiza* in IRISH SEMI-UNCIAL.

I I I I
1 2 3 4

STYLUS: From the Latin *stilus*, an instrument for writing. Made of bone or metal, with a pointed tip used to write on wax tablets. The other end, which was flat, was used for erasing.

SUBSTANCE: The quality of paper based on its weight and thickness. You say that paper "is made with some substance" when it is sturdy and handles well.

TAIL: The lower stroke on certain letters, such as Q, j, p, q. Also called a descender.

TEXTURA: From the Latin *texere* (to weave) (also *textura*, "web"). A GOTHIC script from the fourteenth and fifteenth centuries. It takes its name from the regular structure of strokes and counters within the words. This gives the text a woven pattern. Today, its layout evokes robust tradition, which is why it is often used to advertise products that seek to convey authenticity (cheeses, butcher signs, wines, etc.).

THICK: The thicker strokes of a letter.

THIN: The finer strokes of a letter, also known as hairlines.

TITIVILLUS: Name given in the Middle Ages to the demon of scribes, reputed to cause errors in their transcriptions.

TITULUS: A horizontal line, placed above the letter or group of letters that it is abbreviating. Most often, it marked the suppression of an M or an N.

TOURNEURE: Ornamental UNCIAL letter, used as a majuscule or decorative capital, beginning in the twelfth century. Its design begins with an outline that is then filled in with a quill or brush. Its rounded shape harmoniously complemented the more broken forms of the accompanying GOTHIC letters. It is also called a "versal letter."

TYPE CHARACTER: A lead or brass cube bearing the letter to be printed in relief. Depending on its design and stroke width, the character is considered italic, roman, bold, semi-bold, or light.

b f h k l t

TYPECASE: A rack divided into compartments that hold the typographical characters, arranged in order of how frequently they are used.

TYPOGRAPHY: From the Greek *tupos* (character, impression) and *graphein* (to write).
1. A technique for reproducing texts by assembling and printing characters etched in relief.
2. The graphic shape and style of printed text.

TYPOGRAPHIC RULER: A ruler measuring in Cicero or pica points along one edge and in millimeters or inches along the other edge. It is used for typographical measurements.

UNCIAL: Large capital script, reserved for chapter titles. There are two types of UNCIALS: ROMAN UNCIAL and ARTIFICIAL UNCIAL, which has a more elaborate design. Like ROMAN CAPITAL and RUSTICA, it is used as the uppercase for CAROLINGIAN MINUSCULE.

UPPERCASE: The upper part of a typecase, in which capital letters were arranged. Another name for majuscules.

UPSTROKE: The vertical line extending above the x-height of certain lowercase letters. It is also called an ascender (from the Latin *ascendere*, "to ascend").

VELLUM: From the Old French *veel* (veal). A very fine, high-quality parchment made from calfskin. Also a paper with a pulp base of cotton, with no grain pattern.

VERSO: The back of a sheet of paper, the other side of the recto.

VIGNETTE: Originally, an ornament with branches or vine leaves. In the fifteenth century, the term includes typographical ornamentation used in book decoration. A small illustration.

VISIGOTHIC: In the Middle Ages, the national script of the Iberian Peninsula.

VITRIOL: Another name for ferrous sulfate or copper sulfate. Green vitriol corresponds to ferrous sulfate (also known as *copperas*), while blue vitriol is another name for copper sulfate.

VOLUMEN: A parchment or papyrus manuscript rolled onto a rod. The text is written perpendicular to the rod.

VOLUTE: From the Latin *volvere* (to turn). A spiral stroke. Also a spiral decoration or part of a letter.

VOWELS: From the Latin *vocalis*, from *vox* (voice). The letters whose sound is produced with air escaping freely from the vocal passage. Rimbaud attributed colors to the vowels: *A black, E white, I red, U green, O blue: vowels, / I will recount some day your latent births…*

WATERMARK: The imprint left by a copper or brass thread in the pulp when paper is fabricated, visible when the sheet is held up to the light.

WIRE-MARKS: The ribbing left on paper by the copper wires used in its fabrication.

XYLOGRAPHY: From the Greek *xulon* (wood) and *graphein* (to write). A technique for engraving images and text in relief on wood planks. Another name for wood-cut.

YCIAR: Juan de Yciar. A master calligrapher born in 1522. He authored the famous *Arte Subtilissima*, the first treatise on Spanish writing, published in 1548.

ZOOMORPH: Representing an animal; zoomorphic designs and decorations.

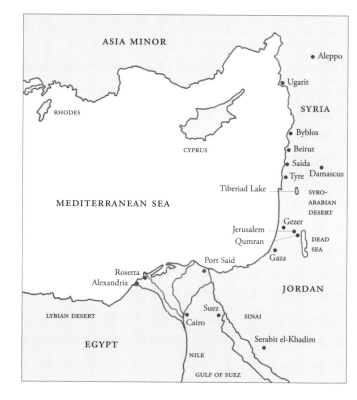

BIBLIOGRAPHY

Abbé Danet, *Grand dictionnaire françois et latin*. Lyon: Deville Freres & L. Chalmette, 1737.

Alphabets, Alphabete, Alfabetos. Paris: L'Aventurine, 2000.

Anderson, Donald M. *Calligraphy: The Art of Written Forms*. New York: Dover Publications, 1992.

Angles, Michel, Siavoch Darakchan, and Mian Sheng Zhu. *Souffle & énergie*. Rodez: Éditions du Rouergue, 1994.

Avril, François. *L'Enluminure à l'époque gothique*. Paris: Bibliothèque de l'Image, 1995.

Baginski, Bodo J., and Shalila Sharamon. *Manuel des Chakras*. Paris: Éditions Entrelacs, 1991.

Beaune, Colette. *Les manuscrits des Rois de France au Moyen Âge*. Paris: Bibliothèque de l'Image, 1997.

Beccaria, Laurent, and Sophie de Sivry. *L'art et l'écriture*. Paris: L'Iconoclaste, 1998.

Berthier, Annie, and Anne Zali. *L'Aventure des écritures, Naissance*. Paris: Bibliothèque nationale de France, 1997.

Bickham, George. *The Universal Penman*. New York: Dover Publications, 1941.

Birren, Faber. *Le pouvoir de la couleur*. Montréal: Les Éditions de l'Homme, 1998.

Blasselle, Bruno. *Histoire du Livre*. Paris: Découvertes Gallimard, 1997.

Bologna, Giulia. *Merveilles & splendeurs des livres du temps jadis*. Milan: France-Loisirs, 1988.

Bonfante, Larissa. *La naissance des écriture: Du cunéiforme à l'alphabet*. Paris: Éditions du Seuil, 1994.

Boucher, Jules. *La symbolique maçonnique*. Paris: Éditions Dervy, 1994.

Bouet, Pierre, and Monique Doscat, eds. *Manuscrits et enluminures dans le monde normand (Xᵉ–XVᵉ s.)*. Caen: Presses universitaires de Caen, 1999.

Breton-Gravereau, Simone, and Danièle Thibault. *L'Aventure des écritures, Matières & formes*. Paris: Bibliothèque nationale de France, 1998.

Calvet, Louis-Jean. *Histoire de l'écriture*. Paris: Éditions Plon and Hachette Littératures, Pluriel, 1996.

Cames, Gérard. *Dix siècles d'enluminure en Alsace*. Strasbourg: Éditions Contades, 1989.

Camille, Michael. *Images dans les marges*. Paris: NRF Gallimard, 1997.

Cazenave, Michel, ed. *Encyclopédie des symboles*. Paris: Le Livre de Poche, 1996. Reprint of *Encyclopédie des symboles féminins* (Paris: Christian de Bartillat, 1980).

Chevalier, Jean, and Alain Gheerbrant. *Dictionnaire des symboles*. Paris: Bouquins/Robert Laffont, 1994.

Christin, Anne-Marie, ed. *Histoire de l'écriture, de l'idéogramme au multimédia*. Paris: Flammarion, 2001.

Combier, Marc, and Yvette Pesez, eds. *Encyclopédie de la chose imprimée.* Paris: Retz, 1999.

de Courson, M., ed. *Cartulaire de l'abbaye de Redon.* Rennes: Amis des archives historiques du diocèse de Rennes, Dol, et Saint-Malo, 1998.

Demeude, Hugues. *Alphabets animés.* Paris: L'Aventurine, 1996.

Diderot, Denis, and Jean le Rond d'Alembert, eds. *L'Encyclopédie: L'Art de l'écriture.* Paris: Chez Briasson, 1751. Reprint, Paris: Inter-livres, 1994.

———. *L'Encyclopédie: Les métiers du livre.* Paris: Chez Briasson, 1751. Reprint, Paris: Bibliothèque de l'Image, 1994.

Dosdat, Monique. *L'Enluminure romane au Mont-Saint-Michel.* Rennes: Éditions Ouest-France, 1991.

Drogin, Marc. *Medieval Calligraphy.* New York: Dover Publications, 1980.

Drucker, Johanna. *The Alphabetic Labyrinth.* London: Thames & Hudson, 1995.

Druet, Roger, and Herman Grégoire. *La Civilisation de l'Écriture.* Paris: Fayard-Dessain and Tolra, 1976.

Duplan, Pierre, and Roger Jauneau. *Maquette & mise en page.* Paris: Éditions du Moniteur, 1986.

Dupuigrenet Desroussilles, François. *Trésors de la Bibliothèque nationale.* Paris: Nathan, 1986.

Étiemble. *L'écriture.* Paris: Delpire, 1961.

Folsom, Rose. *The Calligraphers' Dictionary.* London: Thames & Hudson, 1990.

Frutiger, Adrian. *Des signes & des hommes.* Denges: Éditions Delta & Spes, 1983.

Ghyka, Mathila C. *Le Nombre d'Or.* Paris: NRF Gallimard, 1931.

Glennison, Jean. *Le Livre au Moyen Âge.* Paris: Presses du CNRS, 1988.

Gousset, Marie-Thérèse, and François Avril. *Saint Louis, Roi de France.* Paris: Bibliothèque nationale/Chêne, 1990.

Grégory, Claude, ed. *Encyclopædia Universalis.* Paris: Encyclopædia Universalis France, 1968.

Harris, David. *L'ABC du calligraphe.* Paris: Dessain & Tolra, 1995.

Hoch, Philippe, ed. *Trésors des bibliothèques de Lorraine.* Paris: Association des bibliothécaires français, 1998.

Ifrah, Georges. *Histoire universelle des chiffres.* Paris: Bouquins/Éditions Robert Laffont, 1994.

Irblich, Eva. *Karl der grosse und die wissenschaft.* Vienna: Österreichische Nationalbibliothek, 1994.

Jean, Georges. *L'écriture mémoire des Hommes.* Paris: Découvertes Gallimard, 1987.

Jessen, Peter, ed. *Masterpieces of calligraphy, 1500–1800.* New York: Dover Publications, 1981.

Kandinsky, Wassily. *Point Ligne Plan.* Paris: Éditions Denoël, 1970.

Knight, Stan, and John Woodcock. *A Book of Formal Scripts.* London: A & C Black, 1992.

Kushi, Michio. *Le Livre du Dô-In.* Paris: Guy Trédaniel / Éditions de la Maisnie, 1982.

Landais, Napoléon. *Dictionnaire général et grammatical*. Paris: Bureau central, 1834.

Martin, Henri-Jean, and Jean Vezin, eds. *Mise en page & mise en texte du livre manuscrit*. Paris: Éditions du Cercle de la Librairie-Promodis, 1990.

Masson, Hervé. *Dictionnaire initiatique*. Paris: Jean-Cyrille Godefroy, 1995.

Médiavilla, Claude. *Calligraphie*. Paris: Imprimerie nationale, 1993.

Moscati, Sabatino, ed. *Les Phéniciens*. Milan: Edizioni Bompiani, 1988.

Nicolle, David. *La Vie au Moyen Âge*. Paris: Celiv, 1998.

Ouaknin, Marc Alain. *Les mystères de l'alphabet*. Paris: Éditions Assouline, 1997.

Pächt, Otto. *L'Enluminure médiévale*. Paris: Éditions Macula, 1997.

Reussens, Chanoine. *Éléments de paléographie*. By the author: Louvain, 1899. Reprint, Brussels: Éditions Moorthamers, 1963.

Richaudeau, François. *Manuel de typographie et de mise en page*. Paris: Éditions Retz, 1989.

Roob, Alexander. *Alchimie & mystique*. Köln: Taschen, 1997.

Sacks, David. *Letter Perfect: The Marvelous History of Our Alphabet From A to Z*. New York: Broadway Books, 2004.

Seringe, Philippe. *Les symboles: dans l'art, dans les religions, et dans la vie de tous les jours*. Paris: Éditions Hélios, 1988.

de Souzenelle, Annick. *La lettre, chemin de vie*. Paris: Albin Michel, 1993.

———. *Le symbolisme du corps humain*. Paris: Albin Michel, 1991.

Sterligov, Andreï, and Tamara Voronova. *Manuscrits enluminés occidentaux VIIIe–XVIe s.* Bournemouth: Parkstone, 1996.

Stiennon, Jacques. *Paléographie du moyen âge*. Paris: Armand Colin, 1991.

Stuart, David. "Du signe à l'écriture." *Pour la Science* 33 (October/January 2002).

Tesnière, Marie-Hélène, ed. *Trésors de la Bibliothèque nationale de France*. Vol. I. Paris: Bibliothèque nationale de France, 1996.

Tory, Geoffroy. *Champ Fleury*. Paris: Bibliothèque de l'Image, 1998.

Viers, Rina. *Des signes pictographiques à l'alphabet*. Paris: Karthala/Association Alphabets, 2000.

de Vorepierre, Dupiney. *Dictionnaire français illustré et encyclopédie universelle*. Paris: Bureau de la publication, 1867.

Walther, Ingo F., and Norbert Wolf. *Codices illustres*. Köln: Taschen, 2001.

Zali, Anne. *L'aventure des écritures, La page*. Paris: Bibliothèque nationale de France, 1999.

ACKNOWLEDGMENTS

This work would not have seen the light of day without the assistance and kindness of several people. I would like to extend my most profound gratitude to them. My thanks are especially due to:

—my wife, Sandrine, and Garance, our daughter, for their patience, enthusiasm, and smiles;

—my mother and father, Sylviane and Gabriel, for their warm encouragement and support;

—the whole Éditions Alternatives team: Gérard Aimé, for his trust; Patrice Aoust, Fabienne Lesage, and Catherine Paradis, for the efficient collaboration and kindness; and even more Sabine Bledniak, who was in charge of re-reading the text, for listening, for her judicious advice and her good mood;

—Suzanne Bukiet, who put me in contact with Éditions Alternatives and allowed me to illustrate *La Nuit des Princes*;

—Pascal Sauvestre, for the attention and care that he gave to the first draft of this work;

—David Lozach, for his ability to share;

—Benoît Klein, for his enlightenment;

—Anne Berthier and Anne Zali, for their advice;

—and finally, Sylvie Chokroun, who generously accepted to lend me the Hebraic character that she designed, "The Nathan."